In Memory of

DREW MARTUCCI

FROM
JOAN AND FRED KENNEY

AMERICAN WILDERNESS

photographs
DAVID MUENCH
texts
BERNADETTE GILBERTAS

AMERICAN
WILDERNESS

A journey
through the national parks

VILO

PUBLISHING

Now under the protection of the National Park Service,
nothing troubles the peace of the Tennessee bayous and swamps where the bald cypresses
sink buttress roots into the still waters of Reedfoot Lake.

introduction

The immensity of North America spelled freedom for the immigrants fresh off the ships from Europe. In just a few hundred years, they built this unlimited virgin territory into the economic and industrial superpower we know today. The earth surrendered its mineral resources to the appetite of the industrialists, the forests saw their sap flow under the loggers' axes, the rivers were channelled and the fertile soils exhausted with the effort of feeding millions. Yet despite everything, despite this mistreatment, the Americans never crushed the wild spirit of their land and never humbled its scale. Deeply traumatized by the huge losses of the Civil War, the divided country needed some form of reconciliation. The bloody extermination of the Indian peoples during the conquest of the West, the brutal annihilation of many animal species and the steady transformation of open landscapes into uniform, reticulated holdings were issues that struck a chord across the population, uniting those amazed by the extraordinary beauty of the landscapes they were discovering. It was in this context that the concept of wilderness protection developed and the first national parks were created, a movement given impetus by the philosophers, writers, naturalists and artists of the time, all firmly determined to save the unique character of their natural heritage. The paintings of Thomas Moran and the photographs of William Henry Jackson were so evocative, so convincing, that Congress decided to vote the creation of the first national park, Yellowstone, in 1872. Since this founding date, other parks, monuments, preserves and sites have followed and now blossom in green across the map of the United States. They reflect the astonishing diversity of the country's natural environments. From the Arctic tundra to the Hawaiian volcanoes and including the great prairie, the coral reefs and lagoons, the rocky tablelands and the snowy mountains, most ecosystems are now at least partially protected by a national park. To travel through the American parks is like diving into the geological history of our planet. We follow the great climatic variations which changed the world, discover the extraordinary diversity of the plant world, stand in awe before the world's tallest, heaviest and oldest trees and walk away refreshed by the fragrance of the spring desert flowers. Traveling through the parks, following the alligator along the steamy bayous or tracking the lonely footprints of the grizzly, we rediscover the American wilderness.

■

Antelope Canyon, Arizona.

MAINE

Augusta

VERMONT

Burlington
Montpelier
NEW HAMPSHIRE
Concord

WISCONSIN

LAKE SUPERIOR

St. Paul
lis

LAKE HURON

LAKE MICHIGAN

MICHIGAN

Milwaukee
Madison

Lansing
Detroit

LAKE ONTARIO

Syracuse
Rochester
Buffalo

NEW YORK

Boston
MASSACHUSETTS
Providence
CONNEC-TICUT
RHODE ISLAND

OWA

Des Moines

Chicago

LAKE ERIE

Toledo
Cleveland
Akron
Pittsburg

PENNSYLVANIA

Trenton
Harrisburg
NEW JERSEY
Philadelphia

New York City

ILLINOIS

INDIANA

OHIO

Columbus

Indianapolis

Cincinnati

Ohio

WEST VIRGINIA

MARYLAND
Baltimore
Annapolis
Washington
DELAWARE

Charleston

Louisville
Frankfort

Missouri

Jefferson City

MISSOURI

KENTUCKY

VIRGINIA

Richmond

Norfolk

Mississippi

ARKANSAS

Little Rock

Memphis

TENNESSEE

White

Tennessee

Raleigh

NORTH CAROLINA

Charlotte

MISSISSIPPI

Birmingham

ALABAMA

Montgomery

Alabama

Red

SOUTH CAROLINA

Columbia

Charleston

Atlanta

Savannah

GEORGIA

LOUSIANA

Baton Rouge
New Orleans

Tallahassee

Jacksonville

GULF

OF MEXICO

Tampa
St. Petersburg
FLORIDA
Lake Okeechobee

Miami

ATLANTIC OCEAN

N

scale (except Alaska)

0   100   200   300 km

NATIONAL PARKS

1 ■ THE EAST

1 *Acadia* 2 *Cape Cod*
3 *Cape Canaveral* 4 *Cape Hatteras*
5 *Cape Lookout* 6 *Allegheny*
7 *Great Smoky* 8 *Shenandoah*
9 *Adirondack Mountains*
10 *Congaree Swamp* 11 *Big Cypress*
12 *Biscayne* 13 *Merchants Millpond*
14 *Everglades*

2 ■ THE CENTRAL PLAINS

15 *Isle Royale* 16 *Voyageurs*
17 *Apostle Islands* 18 *Pictured Rocks*
19 *Theodore Roosevelt* 20 *Devil's Tower*
21 *Grand Portage* 22 *Pipestone*
23 *Agate Fossil Beds* 24 *Oglala*
25 *Wind Cave* 26 *Badlands*

3 ■ THE ROCKY MOUNTAINS

27 *Glacier* 28 *Grand Teton*
29 *Dinosaur* 30 *Great Sand Dunes*
31 *Rocky Mountains* 32 *Yellowstone*
33 *White Sands* 34 *Big Bend*

4 ■ THE WEST

35 *Death Valley* 36 *Joshua Tree*
37 *Great Basin* 38 *Organ Pipe Cactus*
39 *Petrified Forest* 40 *Bryce Canyon*
41 *Zion* 42 *Grand Canyon*
43 *Arches* 44 *Monument Valley*
45 *Mesa Verde* 46 *Chaco Culture*
47 *Navajo* 48 *Canyon de Chelly*

5 ■ THE PACIFIC COAST

49 *Channel Islands* 50 *Kings Canyon*
51 *Sequoia* 52 *Yosemite*
53 *North Cascades* 54 *Mount Rainier*
55 *Mount St-Helens* 56 *Lassen Volcanic*
57 *Crater Lake* 58 *Hawaii Volcanoes*
59 *Haleakala* 60 *Olympic* 61 *Redwood*
62 *Oregon Sand Dunes* 63 *Point Reyes*

6 ■ ALASKA

64 *Wrangell St-Elias* 65 *Glacier Bay*
66 *Denali* 67 *Katmai*

Since its discovery, this geyser has never disappointed the visitors who come to admire its impressive spout and clockwork regularity. 'Old Faithful' in Yellowstone National Park.

NATURE AS A WELLSPRING OF THE AMERICAN IDENTITY

Beneath the starry Wyoming sky, the night was already growing chilly in this fall of 1870. Some twenty men were gathered there, around a campfire. It was September 19th and the members of the geological expedition led by Henry D. Washburn and Nathaniel P. Langford had set out a week before from Helena, the capital of Montana. For a week now they'd been exploring the Yellowstone country. On their return, Washburn would recall that "never had the members of one of his expeditions been so captivated by the grandiose spectacle of nature". Fantastic and constantly changing landscapes, churning waterfalls tumbling into canyons with steep, crumbly walls, basins of turquoise water, cauldrons of bubbling mud, ground stained rainbow colors with leaching sulfur, geysers roaring or blowing jets of steam. The expedition had barely approached one of these geysers, baptised 'Old Faithful' because of its regularity, when they were greeted with a huge column of scalding steam and water spouting 120 feet into

the air! That night, at the confluence of the Gibbon and Firehole rivers, the talk grew heated in the firelight. Was it the dancing flames that shone reflected in the eyes of the speakers, or was it the vision of those grandiose landscapes they'd just been through? Some of the geologists were already imagining the mining potential of Yellowstone, but the majority of the expedition had already fallen under the spell of the region. Washburn, in particular, was vigorously opposed to any form of exploitation. Finally, as the fire burned low, when the cigars glowed red in the dark and the whiskey warmed their stomachs, the members of the geological expedition came up with the idea of a campaign to gain federal legislation ensuring the protection of hundreds of thousands of acres of virgin territory and with the further idea of doing everything possible to have a 'public park' created, a park which would be open to everyone. Many expeditions have followed these pioneers. The first photos taken of Yellowstone, by William Henry

Jackson, caused a sensation and favorably influenced the Congress and, on March 1st 1972, Yellowstone was declared the world's first national park. One long night around a campfire was the starting point for a movement to preserve a nation's natural heritage. The story of how North America's national parks were created is the step-by-step story of the protection of an environment so precious to the

principles written into the Constitution began to be challenged. The Civil War, which had violently divided the country by shattering its erstwhile unity, together with the cruelty of the conquest of the West, left traces of doubt and guilt in citizens' minds. Americans of the stature of Washburn began to speak up in favor of public, rather than private, land ownership, thereby inspiring philosophical

American people.

Were they created by chance? Or through the dogged determination of a few nature lovers? And why was it that world's first national parks came into existence in regions open to settlement by millions of immigrants rather than back in their European homelands?

Up until then, this new land had been built on certainties as rock-solid as the country was vast: an almost religious duty to colonize this new 'promised land', be it at the cost of practically unlimited private ownership of the earth, to wipe out the Indians and to irreversibly destroy the animal species such as the buffalo on the great plains. In the middle of the 19th century, the founding

and religious positions regarding the defense of nature. This realization, this consciousness of a heritage, prompted a hasty reflex to protect and safeguard what could still be saved from the greed of the conquerors. And thus it was that the United States of America became the first country to organize a set of measures for the protection of its unspoiled expanses, measures which gradually led to the greening of the map with national parks and monuments, with nature reserves and with state parks. This new conception of protecting natural wildernesses then spread around the globe, in more or less different forms, and today the number of national parks worldwide is estimated at somewhere between 4000 and 5000.

The Gibbon Falls tumble from the high volcanic plateaux
of the Yellowstone park, crimping their flow over the fracture lines.

◁ *The surging plunge of the Lower Yellowstone Falls,*
Yellowstone National Park, Wyoming.

A rare commodity in the Chihuahua Desert,
water runs hidden in the depths of the Santa Helena Canyon ▷
in the Big Bend National Park in Texas.

THE NEW WORLD, A LAND DIVIDED AND WEAKENED

El Dorado, the promised land of milk and honey. The mirage of a new start and a better life, the New World had attracted an ever-growing flow of immigrants determined to flee old Europe and leave its economic problems behind them. The spectacular development of the young American nation from the mid 19th century onwards soon gave rise to violent social and political tensions such as the first strikes of the New England workmen. In 1861, notably, civil war broke out in South Carolina. The so-called War between the States was a fratricidal affair in which Americans fought and killed other

Americans. The human losses were enormous. A real national trauma, the specter of this war long haunted the minds of citizens who no longer wished for anything other than national reconciliation. Yet six years afterwards, the inhabitants of the southern states were still waiting for their civil rights to be restored and racism towards the blacks, and later the Chinese, still ran rife. During these troubled times, the far-off West prompted questions and offered hope. Having bought Louisiana from the French for a handful of dollars, Thomas Jefferson (1743-1826) instructed William Clark and his private secretary, Meriwether Lewis, to explore the uncharted West. The two set off on a trail-blazing expedition which led them, across the Rockies, to the Pacific, whose beating surf they admired in November 1805. Jefferson's project was ambitious. The 'marvelous trail' which the two explorers had just opened was not simply a route to the West. It may have been the trail of exploration, but it was also that of exploitation and despoilment, along which scurried the land surveyors and the trap-

pers. The conquest of the West may have been a dream for millions of Americans, but soon became a synonym for land-grabbing and allotment of a motherland sacred to the Indians.

Wild and refractory. That's how the land appeared to the first pioneers who landed in America. A savage landscape which had been very little modified by the Indians, spread over immense distances. These landscapes were so different from those of Europe... This virgin soil, this *terra incognita,* was so unlike the centuries-old framework of their native land, that their first reaction was apprehension. Moving westwards, the immigrants had managed to cross the Appalachians, that first real barrier between the Atlantic seaboard states and the unknown world of the Indians. They swarmed towards the lands lying further west, pushing back the frontier of the unknown and allowing the nation's territory to expand. This huge migration occupies an important place in the collective American memory and the 'frontier' theme remains a favorite both in the history and the literature of the United States.

The greatest migratory passages in American history took place between 1840 and 1850. To encourage the pioneers to settle farther west, the Homestead Act of 1862 granted a tract of up to 160 acres free to any person of at least 21 years of age wishing to become owner and agreeing to settle and farm his land for at least five years. Thus it became possible for a whole pioneer wave to lay claim to these new territories in the American West. This Homestead Act also led to massive land speculation with the new owners of land acquired literally 'dirt cheap' soon seeking to resell it at a profit. Pushing ever-farther westwards, the pioneers arrived in Indian territory. For these native Americans, who lived in small, drifting groups in perfect harmony with their environment, the notion of land ownership meant nothing. As the fur trade began to develop, rivalries over space began to grow with it. The new immigrants always refused to recognize the Indians' right to the land. They had landed on this new continent as rapacious conquerors and divine providence had offered them free land. It seemed to them quite natural to farm the earth and take possession of it. Yet this vision of things was incomprehensible to the native peoples who couldn't understand how anyone could claim to buy the trees, the rivers, a beach or a lake. Up until the end of the conquest of the West,

Imagined as an Eldorado, a Promised Land,
the New World attracted an ever-growing flood of immigrants looking for a new start and better opportunities.

It was around a campfire like this, out in the wilderness,
◁ *that the idea of national parks first sparked in the minds of an 1870 geological expedition.*

The Oregon National Historic Trail protects the traces
left by the pioneers' wagon trains for over two thousand miles from Independence in Missouri to Oregon City.
Parting of the Ways, South Pass West and ruts in the Wyoming rock.

Threatened with extinction,
the buffalo have now recolonized the plains of Wyoming in Yellowstone National Park.

the relentless struggle against the Indians included the appropriation of their lands and the violation of their rights. The relations between the 'white men' and the 'redskins' were codified in a series of treaties defining the territories of each, treaties which did nothing to prevent a series of bloody battles. On March 3rd 1871, the American government voted the Indian Appropriation Act, invalidating all previous treaties, and the Indians found themselves without any land and without even any status within the American nation.

In the course of this collective drive towards the Pacific, the mining corporations, the railroad

companies and a growing number of individuals were nevertheless eager to find 'green areas' where the general public could go to refresh minds and bodies. The various states then entered the picture, laying their own claims, and it became clear that the State had to reserve, when distributing land, some 'parks' set aside for 'the benefit of the nation and its inhabitants'. Thus we find, for the first time, the use of the term *national* park.

When the first European pioneers set foot on North American soil, the Indian population has been estimated at one million, spread over 600 ethnic groups. Their main preoccupation, in this West where the ecosystems are so fragile, was to 'take care of the earth and the sky'. Their mythology made them one with their often difficult natural environment. The Indians didn't own the land and the land didn't own the Indians. The land belonged to the spirits. President Thomas Jefferson pursued two ambitious but somewhat contradictory objectives for opening the West: making friends with the

cont. page 27

Crossing the Great Plains seemed an endless ordeal for the heavily laden pioneers and their livestock.
Encounters with friendly Indians were generally highly instructive.

*The National Park Service protects the immense diversity of North American landscapes
and many geological curiosities like the hundreds of stone windows in Utah's Arches National Park
and lesser known sites such as Antelope Canyon in Arizona.*

Visiting the Leonard Mine in Butte.

Farewell to Emmy & Koost

Through Montana.

Our Camp at the Flathead Lake.

On a Ferry across the Flathead River.

Once they had conquered the land and claimed its natural riches, the pioneers began thinking about recreation. The national parks were created with this aim also in mind.

Yellowstone Park.

Camp at the Yellowstone Lake.

Start on a 5-Miles Voyage across the Yellowstone Lake.

Building a Raft.

When the official act was signed in 1872, creating the world's first national park,
the 2,221,773 acres of Yellowstone were 'set aside as a public park and place of recreation for the people'.

After sharing Indian tepees for eight years,
the painter George Catlin brought back an impressive portfolio of sketches and oil portraits,
firsthand testimonies to a vanishing way of life.

Indians, so as to develop the fur trade, and finding new land for the pioneers. Yet how could the hand of friendship be extended to the native Americans when the other was taking their lands from them? The fur trade and the trappers were the starting point for a genocide where four-fifths of the original Indian population were slaughtered in the conquest of the West. To satisfy the ever-growing pioneer demand for furs, the Indians moved in quest of new hunting grounds. The violence which characterized the relations between the two populations continued to increase, escalating into rapes, murders and massacres. The Indian peoples, driven backwards, starved and decimated, sought refuge towards the West, often falling victims to the 'silent invasion' of microbes and viruses which the pioneers brought in their wagons. Smallpox, typhoid fever and cholera took their toll on tribes already weakened by the violent conquest of the West. As they crossed the country, the pioneers hunted the big game, notably the buffalo, which was the main source of wealth for most of the Indian peoples. Where the pioneers failed to eliminate the Indians with rifles, the systematic slaughter of the buffalo triggered, in the winters of 1886 and 1887, a famine which destroyed the last pockets of resistance. The end of the 'buffalo god' heralded the end of another world and the Indians saw their ancestral way of life disappear for ever. Even the least hostile finished by hating the whites.

This unfamiliar land, this virgin soil, frightened the pioneers and this fear was certainly the starting point for the great ecological upheavals which traumatized the United States. The conquerors sought to refashion nature as it had been in their native lands, with cultivated fields and well ordered plantations. Thus the era of the great clearances began, together with the introduction of European vegetable and animal species and, indirectly, their parasites. The farmers attacked the major predators to minimize their stockrearing losses. The intensive fur trade led to the disappearance of many predatory species and the consequent proliferation of others. The first explorers who crossed the Rocky Mountains described the fascinating spectacle of whole hillsides seeming to move as herds of pronghorns shifted feeding grounds. By 1920, the numbers of these antelopes, once estimated at 30 million, had fallen to fewer than 15,000. Systematic drives were organized to shoot the wapiti in Canada. Its canines pleased the white fraternity of the Benevolent and Protective Order of the Elks as watchchain decorations. Many species were unable to escape this mass destruction; the Mexican grizzly, the Arizona jaguar, the marine mink and no fewer than eighteen sub-species of North American wolf were totally exterminated, wiped off the map by this intensive hunting. In the sad chapter of this North American carnage, this confrontation of man and nature, the fate of the last passenger pigeon and the slaughter of the buffalo remain written in letters of blood.

President Roosevelt speaking to Sioux leaders in 1903.

THOUGHT AND REASON TO THE RESCUE OF THE WILDERNESS

Paradoxically, the fratricidal wars, the violence, the cruelty and the massacres which tarnished the rapid and brutal conquest of the American continent, were indirectly the starting point for the first environmental protection measures. Indeed, the Americans, still profoundly shaken by the huge losses of the Civil War, wanted to reconcile their

ing in the North American culture, influenced by a line of thinking which gave Nature a predominant role as the hearthstone of civilization, a philosophy which we call transcendentalism. Widely inspired by European Romanticism, this current of thought saw nature as the reflection of spiritual and universal truths which were to nourish both the

divided country. The bloody annihilation of the Indian people, the brutal extermination of many animal species and the progressive transformation of unspoiled landscapes into blandly monotonous plots had to have some effect on a people who were, at the same time, struck by the extraordinary beauty of their natural surroundings and fascinated by the extraordinary tales of the early explorers. Religious factors also played their role, the idea of protecting nature coming more naturally to a Protestant nation, traditionally more inclined than Catholic lands, to respect the works of the Creator. Born of a feeling of guilt and the bitter realization that the damage was irreversible, a new philosophical trend began to make itself heard, more determinedly turned towards nature. Thus the concept of nature took on a quite different mean-

individual and society. For Ralph Waldo Emerson (1803-1882), whose first work 'Nature', published in 1836, made him the figurehead of the Transcendentalists, man had to commune with nature. Another disciple of this philosophy, Henry Thoreau (1817-1862), lived in close harmony with nature throughout his life. A non-conformist by temperament, he pleaded in favor of self-sufficiency, arguing that the headlong pursuit of material possessions reduced the world to slavery. Contrary to the Calvinists, to whom nature opened its doors only to souls purged of all sins, Thoreau stated that nature brought out the best in men and offered them an opportunity of approaching the divine. Nature became, for him, the very symbol of spiritual life, the wellspring of religion. In a famous article dated 1858, Thoreau wrote that

cont. page 35

The delicate sculptures of Utah's Bryce Canyon National Park, carved by wind erosion, seepage water and frost.
Temple Peaks, Bridger Wilderness, Wind River, Wyoming.

Cut into the polished desert sandstone,
these Indian petroglyphs offer tantalizing glimpses of the mysterious 'Ancients'.
Paria River Canyon, Vermilion Cliffs Wilderness, Utah.

Short summer season in full swing in the valleys of Wyoming's Grand Teton National Park. In the space of six brief weeks,
the flowers have to grow, bloom and disperse their seeds before the snows threaten again.

*In California, the Joshua Tree National Monument protects the rare forests
of a strange arborescent yucca which flourishes in this arid, granite-strewn wasteland.*

*Arizona's sedimentary Vermilion Cliffs paint the horizon
against the legendary American 'big sky'.*

"preserving the environment was, to some extent, safeguarding civilization". The following year, he demanded that nature be taken into consideration in towns and suggested creating parks and 'open spaces'. Little by little, transcendentalism opened Americans' awareness to the special quality of their environment. It was better to protect the unique character of the landscapes rather than try to modify them.

Side by side with philosophy, literature also lined up on the side of nature. At the age of 60, the author George Perkins Marsh started writing his 'Man and Nature', a work in which he sought to underline the fragile balance of nature by reference to studies carried out in various countries. Marsh was a member of a group of biological researchers who denounced the environmental abuses of commercial agriculture. His studies had taught him that, without the presence of man, nature was remarkably stable. Marsh didn't believe that man could become an integral part of nature: "Wherever man passes, he sows disorder. When man is involved, the harmony of nature becomes a disaster. No species is as capable as man of killing more than he needs.". When 'Man and Nature' came out in 1863, it was an immediate success. In his own way, Marsh had anticipated the idea of creating protected areas when he wrote that "it is advisable today in North America that vast regions, including the most accessible, remain as long as possible in their original state. Some could serve to teach students, whereas others should remain real jungles so that plants and animals can proliferate there in perfect peace.".

Artists were also suitably impressed by the grandiose American landscapes. Leaving his native eastern homeland, the painter George Catlin (1796-1872) often went west, attracted ever farther by his passion for the Indians. Having spent eight years sharing their life, he brought back a comprehensive folio of oil portraits and sketches. As a painstaking witness of Indian life, he also recorded their surroundings and natural environment. Through his work, Catlin sought to attract as wide a public as possible and alert his spectators to the Indians' need for respect and freedom. During his many stays in the West, Catlin also noted the catastrophic impact of the conquest on the natural environment, "No human imagination,

George Catlin used his paintbrush to claim freedom and respect for the Indians.

even fed by the most wonderful accounts, can picture the beauty and untamed character of the scenes which unfold daily before our eyes in these romantic landcapes.". In 1832, he penned an article in which he proposed the idea of preserving the desert in its most natural state, an idea which tied in with those of the intellectuals and philosophers of the era.

In the course of the 1870s, art was to become - and this time very concretely - the staunch supporter of conservation. This was the period when, through various government expeditions, art became professional. The railroad corporations and the geological surveys were hiring painters, and, more recently, photographers, to have true-to-life pictorial representations of their expeditions. In their own manner and in a deliberately scholastic style, the reports of the early surveys had been drawn up and illustrated by explorers and journalists with real artistic talent. This documentary art, fed by enthusiastic prose descriptions, underlined the unique, fantastic and magnificent character of the natural environment it depicted. Led by Ferdinand V. Hayden, a major geological expedition left the city of Philadelphia in 1871. In his team, Hayden had taken care to include painters whose job was to record the marvels and landscapes of the Yellowstone country. Among these artists was a young local painter named Thomas Moran and the landscape photographer called William Henry Jackson. The latter had loaded his mule with over 200 pounds of equipment including three large-size camera bodies, a considerable number of 8 x 10" glass photographic plates, chemicals, a cumbersome tripod and a darkroom tent! Flexible film hadn't yet been invented and, in the field, Jackson had to go through a laborious rigmarole in his little tent, coating the glass plates with viscous collodion, running out to take his picture as rapidly as possible, taking into consideration that he needed between 5 seconds and 20 minutes exposure time depending on the light, rushing back into his tent to begin development before the collodion dried, washing his plates and finally drying them with a spirit lamp. These were the daily constraints for a photographer of his day, coupled with the difficulties of transport by mule across rugged terrain. It was almost a miracle, under such conditions, that Jackson was able to bring back so many plates intact. His young companion, the painter, better accustomed to salons and studios, also proved that he had a resourceful and resilient streak. Everything was new for Thomas Moran: riding on horseback, camping out in the open air, eating around a campfire... Under the spell, Moran

protection for the region. Nine plates by Jackson and a series of watercolors from Moran went into environmental history that day. The role these works of art played, their influence on the decision taken on March 1st 1872 to protect the Yellowstone region, was unquestionable. Art had taken sides

traveled day after day through what was soon to be the world's first national park, stopping to record the astonishing landscapes. He was particularly impressed by the Yellowstone canyon and by Tower Falls, tumbling down between the narrow banks of a chisel-cut gorge. Back in Washington, Hayden pursued what had become an obsession, battling to persuade still unconvinced congressmen of the need to protect these marvels of nature. Some still didn't believe in the existence of Yellowstone and Hayden carefully chose his proof from among the paintings of Moran and the photographs of Jackson, showing them to Congress while he presented a petition demanding

in the battle of ideas which had been long raging over the recognition of America's natural heritage and its protection. Two huge canvases by Moran were later displayed in the Capitol, reminding city-folk that these sweeping western landscapes were also a part of their country and part of the American legend.

Among the intellectuals and the men in the field, the personality who most influenced the new movement in favor of environmental protection was John Muir, a man whose attachment to nature was a genuine passion. Many heritage sites bear his name today: Muir Lake in Wisconsin, Muir Woods National Monument in California, Mount

cont. page 40

Tipped with their decorative white corollas,
a group of saguaros stand tall in Arizona's Superstition Wilderness.

Mesquite Flat Dunes, in Death Valley National Monument:
the arid heart of North America. California/Nevada.

Art lends Nature a helping hand.
A photograph of Tower Falls tumbling down the volcanic rock walls of Yellowstone and a painting by the artist
Thomas Moran were powerful arguments in the decision to create the world's first national park.

Muir, Muir Peak, the Muir Gorge in Yosemite park and, of course, the famous John Muir Trail which snakes across the peaks of the Sierra Nevada. Born in Scotland, Muir became the unquestionably greatest American naturalist of his time, the greatest, and, having gone to the length of making the great outdoors his home, the least conventional. Following an accident which left him temporarily blind, John Muir chose a way of life entirely focused on nature. He decided to "leave the university of Wisconsin for the great university of Nature.". Throwing a loaf of bread and a handful of tea into his knapsack, he set off, free as air, to travel the American West. When he reached, on foot, the heart of the Sierra Nevada, he sat down to note in his journal that he had achieved the goal that he had long pursued, "to be born again". Traveling through Alaska, he became the first white man to explore the glaciers and the first to demonstrate the glacial origin of Yosemite valley. Indeed, his name remains indissociably linked to the protection of this unique site. He set up camp there for four years, spending his time deciphering the natural mysteries of the valley and guiding the growing volume of tourists. In 1896, Muir and twenty-six other admirers of the valley founded the Sierra Club, an association known as the 'protector of the Sierra' which still militates in favor of environmental protection.

While Thoreau, Emerson and Marsh were, first and foremost, writers, John Muir was the real originator of the 'wilderness' spirit, the foundation stone of the ecological movement.

Through the stands they took and their eloquence, the intellectuals, philosophers, writers, artists and naturalists managed to alert public opinion to the fragility of nature and the need to protect it. Slowly, this idea of nature began to be woven into the American culture. As public awareness dawned, nature became collective rather than private. Men belonged to nature and had the duty to take care of her. The same is true today; nature remains a wellspring of the American identity and 'the American is a man of nature'.

Wisps of blue-tinged fog linger in the valleys of Blue Ridge,
softening the outlines of these age-old mountains. Wayah Bald, North Carolina.

The cold beauty of a purely mineral landscape. Towering above the other peaks
in the Sierra Nevada range, the summit of Mount Whitney captures the first shafts of dawn.
Sequoia National Park, California.

Viewing from Townsend Pass:
Panamint Valley--Argus Range and the
High Sierras in the far background.

Influenced by artistic trends,
philosophical thinking and the writings of naturalists and explorers, Americans feel they belong to nature.
Gradually, down through their history, the concept of nature has blended into the American culture.

Glacier National Park.

Lake Josephine and Mount Gould.

Crossing the Grinnell Glacier.

Grinnell Lake and Garden Wall.

As they were created, one after another,
the national parks were welcomed with increasing enthusiasm.
Backpackers, mountaineers and nature-lovers all flocked to visit the natural wonders of their country.

A sod homestead in Nebraska's Oglala National Grassland.
Oglala is one of the twenty stretches of wild prairie administered by the Forest Service,
tiny islands of what was once a vast sea covering one third of North America.

A halfway house between land and sea, the narrow sliver of land
and delicate string of islands that form Cape Hatteras have their own rich yet fragile ecosystem.
Bodie Island, Cape Hatteras National Seashore, North Carolina.

California's Kings Canyon National Park,
which protects the huge canyons of the Kings River and the peaks of the Sierra Nevada,
was promoted to Biosphere Reserve status in 1976.

Even the bitter winter cold can't quench the fires that heat these basins of water ready to erupt.
West Thumb Geyser Basin, Yellowstone National Park.

In the hushed depths of a snow-blanketed Yellowstone forest, an elk stops to doze.
Energy conservation is vital to survive the rigors of winter.

Photography was required to prove the existence
of the Mammoth Hot Springs formations in the fairytale landscapes of Yellowstone.

Laden with mineral particles, water changes its vocation in Yellowstone.
Instead of wearing away the rocks, it becomes a builder, ▷
creating layers of terraces and basins with delicate lacework brims.

THE AMERICAN WILDERNESS: WILD YET PROTECTED

The word 'wilderness' comes up recurrently whenever Americans talk about nature or when we read books on America's environmental heritage. The dictionary defines this as 'an area essentially undisturbed by human activity' whereas the Bible gives it a desert connotation in the expression 'preach in the wilderness'. The Old English form was *wildeornes,* which indicated, logically enough, a place where *wild deor* (deer) were to be found. Other environmentally descriptive words like tundra or savannah refer to very specific ecological conditions, but the *wilderness,* as quintessentially American as the bush to the Australians, covers a natural wealth of landscapes - desert, forest, jungle, marshland, shoreline or mountain - and a corresponding diversity of fauna and flora. The only common denominator is the absence of human interference.

A constitutional picket fence protects these national treasures today. On a federal level, several State Departments and public bodies share responsibility for management and protection of the American biodiversity. Within the Department of the Interior, the US Fish and Wildlife Service deals with the living creatures, both land and aquatic. It also takes charge of the indispensable task of safeguarding the biotopes and studying the development of the animal species which depend on them. This service also manages the wildlife refuges which, although mostly open to the public, are intended to help conservation. Today's total of 425 refuges covers a total area of 89 million acres. Another bureau of the Department of the Interior, the National Park Service, is charged with administration of the National Parks, Monuments, Historic Sites, Battlefields, Lakeshores, Recreation Areas... and the White House, a total of 374 areas covering some 81 million acres spread over 49 states. The National Ocean Service, governed by the Department of Commerce, is responsible for the marine sanctuaries and reserves located in the estuaries. The National Forest Service manages, within the Department of Agriculture, those federal lands which are largely forested. The states of the union extend this central action and entrust the protection of their heritage lands to specialized public bodies. Some states are proud to include several State Parks, despite the fact that these areas are more for recreation purposes than strict conservation. Private voluntary organizations, like Ducks Unlimited, and prestigious associations such as the Sierra Club and the Audubon Society also contribute their efforts to safeguard America's environmental treasures and today the total acreage of protected natural areas over around 1700 different sites amounts to 18.6% of the land area of the United States, including Alaska, thus ranking America as the world's 6th most protected country. Most of these areas are national and only 2% belong to the states, to the Indian communities or to private organizations like the Conservatory of Nature. In the legal rampart protecting America's heritage land, the notion of National Park remains a keystone.

On March 1st 1872, a mythical date in the history of conservation, Ulysses Grant, 18th President of the United States, signed the official act making Yellowstone the world's first national park. Over two million acres were "set aside as a public park and place of leisure for the people". This first legislative measure failed to give any clear definition of the term 'National Park', but it was a clear success for the movement launched by the naturalists, philosophers, writers and artists. In the face of strong opposition, for whom a federal government wasn't in power to 'breed wild animals', the list of protected sites continued to grow from the early days of the 20th century, gaining momentum in the 1930s during the New Deal. These 'ecological citadels' or 'cathedrals of the New World' became the patrimony of a country without a past and deprived of ancient cultures.

Over a century separates the creation of Yellowstone Park from that of the most recent, California's

*Yucca flowers trace graceful silhouettes
against a pink-tinged sky over New Mexico's White Sands National Monument.*

*The Ajo mountains provide grandstand views over the desert expanses of
the Organ-Pipe Cactus National Monument in Arizona.*

On Signal Hill, in Arizona's Saguaro National Monument,
spiral petroglyphs bear witness to the presence of the Hohokam Indians in prehistoric times.
In the remote mountains of Wind River, up in Wyoming,
the rock illustrates the lives of these first peoples.

Death Valley, promoted from Monument to Park status in 1994. It wasn't until Woodrow Wilson's presidency that a central management organization was created in 1916, the National Park Service, a federal bureau which remains unique. Today, this organization is responsible for some 374 protected sites including National Parks, National Memorials, National Monuments, National Preserves, National Historic Sites and Parks, National Battlefields, Military Parks, Battlefield Parks and Battlefield Sites, National Recreation Areas, National Seashores, Lakeshores, Scenic Rivers and Waterways, National Scenic Trails and other parks covering some 86 million acres of national land.

From the Atlantic to the Pacific, this huge service supervises most of the tourist sites in the United States, from the world's largest known underground labyrinth, Mammoth Cave in Kentucky, to the slopes of North America's highest mountain in

Alaska's Denali Park[1]. From the arctic tundra to the Hawaiian volcanoes, the vast prairies to the lagoons and coral reefs, the desert mesas and the snowy mountains, few American ecosystems remain unprotected by a national park. This extreme diversity makes them difficult to define neatly, but whatever their size and whatever their operating budget, they all attempt to meet the four objectives they have been set: protection, restoration, recreation and scientific research. The protection of the natural environment and the species it contains is an administrative requirement and, as such, gives the parks a legal weight. The restoration of the ecosystems becomes necessary when conservation is no longer enough and where the ecological balance of damaged land must be restored. Certain national parks, for example, launch reintroduction programs for animal or vegetable species which have disappeared. The parks are huge open-air labs for scientific research in geology, biology,

cont. page 57

Looking out from one rim to the other,
the visitor's gaze soars over a labyrinth of mesas and canyons gouged by the Green River.
Green River Outlook, Canyonlands National Park, Utah.

The Mt. Rainier National Park,
Washington.

Mt. Rainier,
from Paradise Camp.

Campsites in the national parks and monuments are always located in magnificent settings.
Paradise Camp at the foot of Mount Rainier. Washington.

Scenes of Bears in the Yellowstone Park.

*For too long, the bears were the principal attraction of the Yellowstone National Park.
Once dependent on handouts, bears often had difficulty in surviving otherwise
and everything is now done to avoid contact between them and humans.*

The Grand Canyon is a theater
with endless stage sets provided by the play of shadow and light across its walls,
veiling and highlighting this most visited of America's national parks.

botany and many other fields. Their protected status allows research programs to be followed up over extended periods. They are also essential 'green lungs' for nearby townships, areas where people can practise their favorite outdoor activities such as camping, backpacking, rock-climbing, contemplation, animal-watching and learning about nature. The parks develop teaching programs on these themes, lay out guidance trails, put up information boards and organize exhibitions, campfire discussions, outdoor filmshows and other educational activities.

The parks now are victims of their own success. Over the past thirty years, the number of visitors has more than tripled to almost 300 million today. Yet for the history of environmental protection, they remain, as the British ambassador James Bryce put it, "the best idea America ever had".

'previously Mt McKinley National Park

The first flickers of early fall sunlight on Mount Seaford in Alaska's Wrangell-St. Elias National Park.

The Grand Teton range rises in a spectacular rock wall from the Wyoming plains,
its jagged peaks forming a daunting introduction to the Rockies.

*Was there other land
on the far side of this seemingly
insurmountable wall?
St Mary Lake, Glacier National Park.*

A JOURNEY
THROUGH THE NATIONAL PARKS

A GEOGRAPHICAL OBSTACLE COURSE FOR THE PIONEERS

An area of over 3.6 million square miles, 2800 miles from east to west and 1200 from north to south, with some 88,000 miles of tidal shoreline, the raw figures give us the scale of this subcontinent. The topography and the geological formations form great masses and the relief lines run parallel to the meridians of longitude.

In 1892, Elisée Reclus summed up the geography of the United States as follows, "The American territory features a remarkable simplicity of construction: it is a vast median plain, having the Mississippi river as sinuously winding axis, and two mountain systems as outer edges". For a person on foot, on horseback or on a covered wagon, it seems a lot less simple. Only courage and unlimited faith allowed the pioneers on their way west to cross the mountains, the vast plains, the desert and the great rivers.

The accessible Atlantic seaboard, with its succession of lagoons and its southern chain of keys, had offered easy anchorages to the European ships. The coastal plain, narrow in the north, progressively widens towards the south, until it reaches the coral peninsula of Florida, and covers all the edge of the Gulf of Mexico. The hard sedimentary layers form vast amphitheaters which separate highly fertile silt-laden depressions. This welcoming and well-protected region was ideal for the first immigrants and allowed continued exchanges with their native homelands. But for those who, tempted by the great adventure of the West, set off into the unknown, the difficulties were about to begin. With the coastal plain behind them, they first had to cross the fall line, that first clean break in the slope, before tackling the rocky glacis rising progressively towards the inland barrier of mountains. The deep ravines cut into this terrain by the abundant water gushing down the slopes of the Appalachians did little to help the progress of their heavily laden wagons. Veined with minerals and

61

From east to west,
relief lines like these worn Appalachian highlands run parallel to the meridians.
Spruce Knob on Seneca Rocks, West Virginia.

coal reefs, these well watered and well drained uplands were soon recognized as prime urban and industrial development sites. For those pioneers who continued inland, the seemingly endless slope finally stopped at the first escarpments of the Appalachians. This chain of mountains rises in the flatlands of the Gulf of Mexico and runs north, parallel to the Atlantic, for over 1800 miles, crossing the Canadian border, continuing up through Nova Scotia and finally dwindling to its end on the island of Newfoundland. The Appalachians are a primary, or Paleozoic, range, folded and leveled by erosion and then dislocated by great fracture lines. Some of the pioneers despaired of ever finding a pass across this great wall of rock and, tempted by

the sense of protection offered by these fertile slopes, preferred to unhitch their wagons and settle there. They started building and soon established a whole series of small rural communities. The Mohawk basin opened the way to the Great Lakes and the Hudson valley. The West finally became accessible from the Atlanta indentation, up the Mississippi and then the Ohio and, especially, over the Cumberland Gap.
From the other side of the Appalachians, the landscape stretched flat and featureless to the far horizon. The central basin, which the Easterners called the Great Desert, covers almost a third of the United States. Only a few crests of hard rock stand out above the thick layer of sediments deposited there

cont. page 65

Water is spread unequally over the North-American continent.
The Californian coastline is supplied from inland sources such as Mono Lake.
Out west, water is a rare and precious commodity, hidden in the depth of canyons
such as those in the Big Bend National Park, Texas.

Michigan's Porcupine Mountains offer visitors panoramic views over the Appalachian forests.
Created in 1972, Missouri's Ozark National Scenic Riverway was the first protective measure of its kind ▷
established to preserve the landscapes along certain rivers.

in the primary era. As they snailed their way west, the pioneers found little to reassure them. The Black Hills gave way to the Badlands and the prairie grasses, sometimes six feet high, were like wading through water. The winters were bitterly cold and the summers hot and humid. Continual Indian presence was an additional strain and the feeling

through a rich bed of alluvial soil before separating into a wide delta as it reaches the Gulf of Mexico, some 2500 miles farther south. As the plains stretch southwards, the landscape becomes more rugged and the relief more abrupt.

Beyond the great river, the High Plains crumple into folds as they run into the Rockies and gradu-

of insecurity grew as they advanced into this open, infinite landscape where the waving grass reached up to touch the scudding clouds. Yet despite appearances, the Great Plains were made up of a mosaic of different environments. To the north lay the contact zone between the old platform of the 'Canadian shield' and the richer sedimentary lands. The Great Lakes, themselves surrounded by myriad smaller lakes, are the reminders of the power of Quaternary glaciers which first scoured the land and then left huge morainal deposits as they retreated. The valleys follow shallow curves and the rare uplands are merely gentle hills. One of the world's longest rivers, the Mississippi, has its headwaters in this region. Its lazy flow meanders

ally begin to rise until, at their highest, they reach 6000 feet. This imposing wall of mountains, studded with 64 peaks like watchtowers, stretches for 3000 miles from northern Mexico, up through Canada, to Alaska where it culminates, at 20,320 feet, with Mount McKinley (or Denali), the highest mountain in North America. In the 18th century, the Rockies were a nightmare for the explorers who attempted to find a path across the sparkling slopes they had seen from afar on the Great Plains. Access was slow and difficult. The frontiersmen, the trappers and the mountain men found new employment as trail blazers and guides. The Walker pass towards northern California and, especially, the southern Smith pass became the golden gateways

*Undisturbed peace and calm
is a guaranteed commodity in the northern lakes of the United States.
Voyageurs National Park, Minnesota.*

for millions of immigrants flooding west.

Geological history fashioned the Rockies in a series of chains separated by valleys and basins. Ice-age glaciers filed down the summits, gouged out cirques and widened the valleys while volcanic activity contributed to the chain's renewal. Earthquakes remind us today of the seething forces under the earth's crust in this region. It was in these grandiose landscapes that the first national parks were created.

Heaven or Hell? What were the pioneers to find west of the watershed of the Rockies? As they discovered, the far side fell away in a series of benches forming vast tablelands and basins. To the north, the Columbia plateaux are covered with great lava spills sculptured by the glaciers while, to the south, lies the Great Basin, a region of desert depressions separated by rugged mountain chains. This southern landscape is a textbook example of wind erosion where the sandstone rock is slowly abraded and deposited in shifting dunes. This driest region of the United States is enclosed upon itself; its hydrographic network has no outflow to the sea. This geographic peculiarity gives birth to many lakes, most of them temporary, including the largest of all, the Great Salt Lake. In 1846, the first of a selection of 1500 Mormon pioneers crossed the frozen Mississippi in an exodus which, within scarcely more than two decades, led some 80,000 refugees to the Great Salt Lake valley where, reassured by the very unattractiveness of the site, they felt safe to build their Zion. This first pioneer train of 171 souls arrived in July 1847 under the leadership of Brigham Young, senior member of the Council of the Twelve Apostles, and began the construction of Salt Lake City. Farther south, the sandstones of the Colorado plateau are deeply ravined by the waterflow networks. This is the land of the canyons. In the Grand Canyon national park, the most visited natural site in the United States, the Colorado river has carved a mile-deep gorge, four to eighteen miles wide, through the successive geological strata.

Before reaching the distant Pacific coast, the pioneers had still a final barrier to cross or circumvent. Starting around the Canadian border, the Cascades spur down from the curving spine of the Rockies, culminate in the isolated volcanic peak of Mount Shasta (14,162 ft) before leaving the stage to the Sierra Nevada, which runs due south to the gates of Los Angeles, blocking the advance of the Nevada deserts. Carpeted with luxuriant damp forests, the Cascades owe their name to the many

cont. page 70

Water abounds everywhere in the state of Michigan.
Tahguamenon Falls State Park.

The diversity of North America also shows in the variety of its plant life. Ancestral trees, like the bristlecone pine, survive unaffected by the rigors of the climate. Bristlecone pines from the Great Basin and whitebark pines on the shores of Crater Lake, Oregon.

As it cools, the liquid lava spilling from Idaho's Craters of the Moon region twists into furrows and ropes.

Basalt columns in the Devil's Postpile National Monument in California

waterfalls which come tumbling down from their volcanic peaks and metamorphic domes. In the south, down the length of California, the all-granite Sierra Nevada reveals its splendor in the Yosemite, King's Canyon and Sequoia National Parks. Between this western cordillera of the Rockies and the Coast Ranges lies a deep trench leading, at its northern end, into the Pacific through the twisting fjords of the Puget. The much wider Californian valley, now one of the country's most fertile regions, is a recent sink zone. Lying along the San Andreas fault, it represents the tectonic frontier between the North American plate and the North Pacific plate. The Pacific ocean and the south west-

ern part of California are gradually moving north west with regard to the American continent as a whole and, in time, California is doomed to drift off from the mainland like a raft into the ocean. From the pioneers' point of view, the geography of the United States was rather like an obstacle course featuring a series of outsize difficulties. Each pass, each valley, each landscape - even the smallest rifts and fissures - played a role in the conquest of the west. *"Forty years of wanderings, in the harshest conditions, led the American explorers towards the farthest horizon open to their courage, the Pacific ocean[2]".* The promised land of the immigrants had moved from one ocean to another.

[2]*Histoire du Far West,
J.L. Rieupeyrout,
Tchou, 1967*

*The slopes of Hawaii's Haleakala crater are peppered with silversword,
a plant that grows nowhere else but in this park.*

*The ocotillos, a species of candlewood, raise their thorny arms
along the sides of the Sierra Del Carmen in Big Bend National Park, Texas.*

*White Sands National Monument protects most of this huge sea of gypsum dunes,
home to various species of plants and animals which have adapted their coloring
to suit the dazzling environment. New Mexico.*

Whipped by the waves, sea foam lies like snow on the ocean.
Olympic National Park, Washington.

*Along the continent's extreme westerly edge, the Pacific coastline
is battered by the ocean rollers. Trees uprooted by the waves are later thrown up on the shore.
Olympic National Park, Washington.*

The warm, dry climate of the semi-desert western regions
suits the towering organ-pipe and cholla cacti in Arizona's Organ-Pipe Cactus National Monument
and the spiny yucca in the gypsum soil of White Sands National Monument in New Mexico.

SAGUAROS, MANGROVES AND SEQUOIAS: NATURE IN MANY GUISES

Bordered by two oceans and open to the four winds, the United States is subject to all climatic influences. The central depression, flanked by its mountain ranges, becomes a corridor. Masses of warm, humid air billow up from the Gulf of Mexico and the tropical regions of the Atlantic only to clash with the glacial winds sweeping down from the Arctic ocean. Masses of cold, dry continental air swirl down from Canada to invade the central part of the land, while warm, dry air from Mexico gives the south-west its semi-arid climate. The influence of marine currents creates further climatic diversity. While the Gulf Stream warms the Atlantic coast from Florida to North Carolina, the Labrador current chills all the north-eastern seaboard and the southern part of the Californian coastline is governed by another cold current which inhibits all rainfall.

The mountain ranges stop the rain clouds from moving inland. The eastern flanks of the Appalachians are generously watered with rain from the Atlantic but the sheltered, western slopes remain dry. The Rockies play the same role on the other side of the country. A temperate climate reigns over all the United States but the marked contrast in the seasons and the sometimes violent climatic passages are often surprising. In the High Plains, the frequent whirlwinds increase the effect of erosion. Fogs of rare density blanket the north-east and the Appalachians. In California, the ocean mists and the pollution combine to give Los Angeles the finest and reddest sunsets in the Far West. Alabama sometimes shivers in waves of cold and flooding is frequent in the Mississippi corridor.

Pot-bellied saguaros, spiny prickly pears, knotted junipers, ancient bristlecone pines, waving buffalo grass, steamy mangroves, bald cypresses, giant mountain sequoias, redwoods towering in the mists, dwarf willows and Arctic lichens... North American diversity is an understatement. In the east, the forests are higher, greener and more exuberant than in the Old World, their undergrowth tangled with clinging vines. Yet the difference is not astonishing. The great stands of oak, maple, beech and lime are reminiscent of the deciduous forests of Europe. The wet continental climate assiduously waters the woods of the Atlantic northeast and the huge Appalachian forest. Behind the flaming reds of the mixed maple woods in the late Indian summer loom the black and white bulk of the spruce, the balsam fir and the smooth straight boles of the aspen. They trace the banks of the Great Lakes and carpet the slopes of the moraines. The taiga, or subarctic forest, begins where the tundra ends. Here the conifers, the spruce and the Banks pine spring from an undergrowth of berry bushes. Farther south, along 2250 miles of the Pacific coast from Alaska to northern California, a gentler maritime climate provides the rainfall required to sustain the most astonishing vegetation in the temperate world, a forest of such profusion and on

such a gigantic scale that it compares with a tropical rainforest. Yet its relatively simple composition, dominated by the Douglas fir, the giant thujas and the Sitka spruce, indicates a closer kinship with the northern forests. The deep green of the conifers underscores the fluorescence of the hanging vines and the undergrowth. Still farther south, the Sequoia sempervirens or redwoods reach heights of 360 feet, their lower branches swathed in the cold mists of the Pacific. The forest and the ocean intermingle so closely here that the mink, a little land carnivore, adds crab to his diet while the marbled murrelet, a tiny wave-surfing bird, flies in to nest in the tops of the sequoias. The coastal plain, from Virginia in the east to Texas, is remarkable for its exclusively American flora. While the ranks of pines occupy the distant horizon, the forests down by the shoreline and along the Mississippi floodplain have a more secret, impenetrable character which verges on the exotic.

*A sea of early-morning mist blankets the Lake
of the Clouds in Michigan's Porcupine Mountains Wilderness State Park.*

*The gentle maritime climate in the west provides the moisture
required to fuel the development of an astonishing temperate rain forest brimming with vitality.
Back east, the great Appalachian forest is mostly composed of hardwoods which, just before the fall,
burst into a spectacular Indian summer blaze of color.*

Strange wooly-looking cypresses sink their buttress roots into the swamp waters. Spanish moss hangs its gray-green filaments from all the branches of these phantoms wandering in the labyrinth of the bayous. And finally, the mangroves fringe the coral reefs of Florida, marking the tidal range of the Atlantic and offering, with their stilt-like roots, strategic perches for the egrets and other wading birds.

The forests have chosen the best soils and the best situations, abandoning the heart of the country, the Great Plains, to the prairie. This region today bears little resemblance to the land the pioneers encountered. Broken up by the plow, exhausted by years of intensive and extensive agriculture, exposed to the erosive action of the winds, criss-crossed with fencing, perforated with derricks drilling for black gold and eaten away by the spread of industrial cities, it has changed completely. Fortunately, national parks and monuments now protect great belts of grassy emptyness. In subtropical Florida, the prairie enjoys a generous rainfall lacking in the central states, and soon transforms itself into swampland. In the Everglades park, the prairie, made up of saw grasses which cut like razors and stand up to practically hurricane winds, becomes one huge, slow-flowing river. These Florida marshlands are home to the American wood stork, the rare American crocodile and its cousin, the alligator. The tundra, another type of openland vegetation, but in the cold regions, forms a sort of plant buffer zone between the taiga and the silent world of the glaciers. This treeless zone is carpeted with a low, shrubby vegetation, composed mainly of dwarf willow and birch, spreading heather, lichens and mosses, all specially adapted to offer the least resistance to the sweeping arctic winds. This is the land of the caribou, the New World reindeer and king of the tundra with its broad, spreading hooves designed for trekking across the water-logged, frozen and slippery terrains.

Plateaux of sandstone as smooth as a tabletop, vertical lines of sheer cliffs, gentle slopes rubbed into giant staircases by erosion, hillsides worn away to leave a landscape of voluptuous sculptures, chaotic fields of jumbled blocks and needles of rock, reliefs like the ruins of ancient cities and huge towers of sandstone looming up from wide valleys... these are the landscapes of the West, the archetypal settings for all westerns. Despite their landscapes more mineral than vegetal, these semi-arid regions are in fact a rich and varied environment. The vegetation has had to adapt to the burning heat, to

Wind erosion sculptures.
Monument Rocks, Smoky Hill River, Kansas.

the exposure and to the irregular rainfall. The mesquite and the creosote bushes limit evaporation with their spiny foliage while the cacti and Joshua trees grow protective spines.

The scale, both in longitude and latitude, of North America implies a great variety of climates which, in turn, give rise to a remarkable range of natural environments. From the coral reefs to the vast rolling prairies and the frozen tundra, not forgetting the twisting bayous and the scorching canyons, the discovery of the United States is a series of contrasts.

Living with its roots in the waters of the Okefenokee swamp in south-east Georgia, the bald cypress, one of the rare deciduous conifers, owes its name to its bare appearance in winter.

The sun travels its course from one side to the other of the Grand Canyon,
highlighting the domes, temples and minarets before abandoning them to the shadow world for another day.
South rim, Grand Canyon National Park, Arizona

1

THE EAST

From boreal forest to tropical swamps

"As the years go by,
the forest that we don't see changing
in fact dances to a slow melody of opportunity and adaptation,
waltzing with time to rhythms of change."

David Middleton,
contemporary American photographer, writer and naturalist

From April through August, the rhododendrons,
◁ *magnolias and tulip trees reveal their true splendor in the misty depths of the Appalachian forest.*
Blue Ridge Parkway, Virginia.

Freed by the erosion of softer rocks around it,
this block of quartz once tumbled down the slopes of the Great Smoky Mountains,
now covered with fir and spruce forests.

On September 6th 1620, one hundred and two men, women and children set out from Plymouth in England on board the Mayflower. They were religious dissidents, seeking to escape the religious pressure of the Stuarts and the Puritans, looking to found a New Jerusalem where they would be free to worship. After a stormy ten-week crossing, they landed on the shores of Massachusetts. This promised land flowed with neither milk nor honey; the dark impenetrable forest ran as far as the eye could see, watered by the abundant rainfall and the first winter was so long and harsh that half of the colony died before spring. Yet with obstinacy, courage and an almost despotic rigor, the pilgrims gradually cleared the woods, drained the land and culti- vated their crops, establishing an economically stable colony from the chill Appalachians down to the steamy south. Since these early days, despite spreading urbanization all down the eastern seaboard, the forest has regained its status as a natural heritage. The eastern national parks protect an astonishing vegetal diversity which ranges from boreal taiga through gallery forests and aquatic plant forms down to subtropical mangroves.

The well-named Great Smoky Mountains swathed in their characteristic morning mists.
Tennessee/North Carolina.

Ghostly forms of bald cypresses mirrored in the marshy waters
of Merchants Millpond State Park, North Carolina.

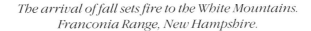

The arrival of fall sets fire to the White Mountains.
Franconia Range, New Hampshire.

NEW ENGLAND: THE TREE AND THE WAVE

The beating heart of the pioneers' new world, New England, has managed to stay wild and natural. Despite its long colonial history, the proximity of urban megalopoles like New York and Boston and its booming economic development, this region, made up of the six states of Massachusetts, Maine, New Hampshire, Vermont, Connecticut and Rhode Island, has a population of barely 15 million. In the inland parts of Vermont, Maine, Connecticut and New Hampshire, originally 95% wooded, the logging was so intensive that the laurentian forest covered only a quarter of the land in the mid 19th century. Yet the forest was more tenacious than the most determined lumberjack or farmer and has now regained most of its former territory. The only traces of this rough past when men tried to grow wheat and corn in the poor soil and harsh climate are the old stone walls, stretching like the bleached bones of a long-dead agricultural landscape. The great white pines of the boreal forest may have disappeared, commandeered by the British Navy for shipbuilding, but today's forest is otherwise in good condition. Nothing is left of the primary woods, of course - every acre has been cut at least once - but the regrowth is impressive. In Maine, the endless forest is the kingdom of the paper-makers, anxious to preserve their source of raw material. Thus we find the strange paradox of a region where highly developed industry (the 'pine tree state' is one of the world's largest pulp-paper producers) guarantees the protection of the natural landscape. New England's favorite time of year is the so-called 'fifth season' or Indian summer, that sacred moment in the fall, towards late September, when every tree and every leaf participates in a collective blaze of color. The spectacle, known simply as 'the color', is never the same from one year to the next but always attracts crowds. The explanation for this spectacle is still unclear; is it the combination of cool nights and sunny days? The quality of the air? Or the chemistry of the soil? The newspapers even publish daily reports to allow visitors to follow the outburst of color from one region to another. In Baxter park, Maine's highest point, Mount Katahdin (5,268 ft), looks down powerless on the raging flames which encircle it. The sumacs light the spark when their yellowing leaves flare crimson in late August. The marsh maples are next, turning a deep cherry red. The Virginia creepers, the white ash and the black ash catch fire in turn. The birches glow bright yellow while the sugar maples shine pinky-red. Only the conifers resist, protected by their deep green fire-proof suits. Fanned by the wind, the fallen leaves pile up like still-glowing sparks while the brown oaks, glowing bronze and purple, add a final touch to the blaze. Only the waves of the Atlantic are strong enough to put out the fire of this wild Indian summer. Over to the east, the ocean hurls itself against the jagged rocks and high cliffs of pink granite. This wild and indented coast has been chosen as a vacation destination by discreet millionaires attracted by its natural beauty. These landcapes must have reminded the early pilgrims of the rough coasts of Devon and Cornwall they had sailed from. Towards the south, the shoreline softens into beaches which stretch for miles out onto a long, curving peninsula where the conifers finally give up. Cape Cod, the departure point for the northern fishing fleets, remains impregnated with the memory of its whaling days.

The beaches of Cape Hatteras,
in North Carolina, gilded by the early morning sun
and swept clean by the rollers of the Atlantic.

Its lush forests, nourished with generous rainfall,
explain why the early French settlers baptized this state Vermont, literally the 'Green Mountain'.
Big Brand Wilderness, Green Mountains.

The Appalachian Trail, running across the peaks from Maine down to Georgia, ▷
is the best way to discover the unspoiled depths of the Great Smoky Mountains.

*Fiery autumn colors rage in New Hampshire while spring brings
a symphony of greens to the well-watered forests of the Great Smoky Mountains.*

*The Indian summer, that magic moment just before the fall
when every leaf and every tree participates in what New Englanders simply call 'the Color'.
Upper Kennebec River Valley, Maine.*

THE SUGAR MAPLE, QUEEN OF THE INDIAN SUMMER

One tree is accused of setting fire to the magnificent eastern American forests. Every fall, the sugar maple and the twelve other species of native North American maples are responsible for the multicolored blaze of the Indian summer. It is also the most tolerant of its family as regards lack of sunlight, growing readily in the shadow of other hardwoods or conifers. In the maple groves, the ground is carpeted with plantlets waiting their turn. When an old tree falls at the honorable age of 250, a

youngster immediately takes its place, growing rapidly for the first forty years of its life. Once an adult, it begins to produce thousands of winged seed, technically known as samaras, every year. Only a few of these keys will sprout. The Latin name for the maple, acer, means sharp, a reference to its hard, close-grained wood, particularly prized in North America for fine cabinetwork. It's at the end of the winter that the maple gives the best of itself, offering its life-giving sap which the Amerindians taught the white settlers how to tap. A cut in the trunk allows harvesters to collect the precious sweet sap which, once boiled and concentrated, produces maple syrup and sugar. An adult maple can give 65 gallons of sap a year, enough to make over ten pints of maple syrup or five pounds of sugar. Given all these qualities, perhaps it's not surprising that the maple's five-pointed leaf was chosen to feature on Canada's national flag.

Later destined to turn pink, before flaming to cherry red, this maple extends its golden autumn foliage over the Ellis River in New Hampshire's White Mountains.

*Maple leaves glow like stars in the falling dusk
over the Blue Ridge Parkway in Virginia*

The dense pelt of conifers grows right down to a shoreline
where long-gone glaciers deposited this erratic boulder in Maine's Acadia National Park. Base Harbor Head.

The peat beds and heaths of the Acadia National Park
bear witness to the harshness of the climate and the scouring cold of Maine's north wind.

Granite cliffs and sandy beaches succeed one another along the Atlantic seaboard.
Acadia National Park, Maine.

The ocean waves chisel down the forbidding cliffs and patiently polish ▷
the granite pebbles along the Acadia National Park seashore.

THE BLUE LINE OF THE APPALACHIANS

Worn and pleated like an accordion, the Appalachians form an enormous barrier, 300 miles wide and over 1800 miles long, stretching from Newfoundland down to Alabama. The base, rising gently from the coastal plain, is now mainly covered by cities and cropland. The longitudinal valleys have become communication links between the north and the south, but the forest is still alive and flour-

of Shenandoah, daughter of the stars. This name was also given to the national park which, since 1926, protects the upper part of the Blue Ridge mountains and the exceptional wealth of wildlife it contains. Running through the park, scenic Skyline Drive offers visitors magificent views over the eastern foothills and the Shenandoah Valley. It cuts across the Appalachian National Scenic Trail, the

ishing on the poor soils of the Allegheny plateau and the skyline crests. The Appalachian forest is a forest of broad-leaved trees on a vastly larger and richer scale than those the European colonists had left behind them. It contains species, such as the sweet gum, the hickory, the orange-flowered tulip tree and the sweet-scented magnolia, which they had never seen. Its undergrowth is dense, encumbered with lianas like wild vines, and it thrives on the warm rain and the snows which fall all year round on the summits and notably on Blue Ridge, the highest and most undulating of its crestlines. The Blue Ridge mountains are so often swathed in mist that the Indians gave them the poetic name

famous backpacking pathway which snakes over 1800 miles from Maine down to Georgia along the crest of the Appalachians and ends shortly after having crossed the Great Smoky Mountains National Park. The Smokies are at their best in the spring, garlanded with flowers. From April through August, the rhododendrons, magnolias, mountain laurels and orchids compete in an outsize floral show. Over the past few years, the name of the Great Smoky Mountains has gained another, less agreeable signification from the reduced visibility caused by the sulfur and hydrocarbon emissions from what is one of the most industrialized and urbanized regions of the United States.

Notes of autumn on Jordan Pond in Maine's Acadia National Park.

The crests of the Blue Ridge Parkway paint a shimmering blue horizon above the hazy morning mists of the Appalachians. North Carolina.

A natural barrier, the Appalachians collect abundant rainfall
and send it cascading back down to the valley floors.
Rainbow Falls, Great Smoky Mountains National Park, North Carolina/Tennessee

Up on West Virginia's Spruce Knob Top,
searing winter temperatures fracture these rocky outcrops.

Sparkling with dewdrops,
a cobweb filters the dawn rays in Pennsylvania's Allegheny National Forest.

The sun sets over a country road between fields
opened for agriculture in the Allegheny National Forest, Pennsylvania

*Helping the trees to breathe in their waterlogged environment,
these peculiar knees rise from the roots of the bald cypresses to break the surface
of Merchants Millpond in North Carolina's state park.*

BORN UNDER A WATER SIGN

Tropical languor, sun-kissed beaches, motionless rivers... as if suspended in time, the tropical south invites idleness. Yet despite this outwardly calm appearance, the south is a battlefield for warring natural elements. Land and water grapple in an age-old fight while fresh and salt water struggle for dominance. Here, in the Gulf of Mexico, the world's third longest river, the Mississippi-Missouri, ends its interminable 3880-mile course. Undecided and lazy, the Mississippi and its companion, the Atchafalaya, wind across a flat plain in endless meanders which combine to form the famous Louisiana bayous, those labyrinths of still water fringed with luxuriant greenery. Hanging from the trees, rooted in the earth or surging from the still

waters, fragile or indestructible, this vegetation takes all sorts of forms. Spanish moss, lianas, water plants, algae and lichens drape the bayous. The smooth, majestic trunk of the bald cypress towers out of the water, supported by the 'kneeling pilgrims' of its strange buttress roots. The bald cypress would not look the same without the hanging garlands of its Spanish moss, an epiphyte which derives its nutrients from the air and prevailing humidity. Georgia's Okefenokee swamp and the White River swamp in south east Arkansas, now national reserves, protect some very ancient cypresses, reputed to be somewhere between 600 to 700 years old, spared from the axes of lumbermen in quest of roof shingles. On its way to the

*The shell-strewn beaches of Cape Canaveral State Park
are convincing proof of the rich natural environment. Florida.*

*Sea oats colonize the sandy shores of Santa Rosa Island
in Florida's Gulf Islands National Seashore.*

sea, the Mississippi accumulates debris washed from the over-farmed land of the central plains farther north, carrying it down to its gigantic delta. Every year, over 800 billion tons of solid deposits are left in this delta where the country has a strange amorphous feel: neither solid nor liquid but somewhere between - the sort of territory that the mangrove prefers.

Born of the sea, sediment upon sediment in ancient geological times, Florida stretches like a finger into the Atlantic. Washed by the sea on almost all sides, lashed by cyclones and hurricanes from the ocean, dotted with lakes and criss-crossed with slow-moving rivers, the waterlogged peninsula barely manages to keep afloat. Even today, the struggle between the land and water is still unfinished. The mangroves steal a march on the sea, the ocean tears away the coast, the tall grasses choke the rivers and man exhausts both. This most southern of all the states still enjoys a temperate climate in its northern parts. As we move farther south, the pine forests and then the dry savanna give way, as the tropical climate makes itself felt, to a world of brackish water.

The Spanish moss trailing from the branches of the Suwannee River live oaks
is in fact an epiphyte or air plant, growing on the host but deriving its nourishment from the air and humidity.
Okefenokee Swamp, Georgia.

The bald cypress develops these spreading buttress roots
to maintain its footing in the unstable swamp environment.
Reelfoot, Tennessee.

THE ALLIGATOR, GUARDIAN OF THE SWAMPS

The water lies like a sheet of glass in a world of absolute silence and stillness. Not a ripple disturbs its surface. The beaming round face of the sun can disappear at last. The still water mirrors the sky and the black silhouettes of the bald cypresses. An atmosphere of general lethargy reigns over the swamp when a sudden roaring rends the silence. Ten seconds later the sound reverberates again, a powerful, gutteral bellow, intense as a small airplane engine. Tonight, again, the alligator sends out his love call. And the sound is infectious; most of his neighbors, both male and female, follow his example. Soon the swamp is in turmoil. This is spring, and when the alligators meet to mate, the bellows last anything from ten minutes to half an hour. A trained observer can distinguish the voice of each alligator in a given territory and

scientists believe that the animals can themselves distinguish friends and foes. The American alligator is the most vocal of the crocodilians. His performances are no doubt adapted to his environment, to the dense, enclosed vegetation which surrounds him. *Alligator mississipiensis* is only found in North America, from the coastal plains of Virginia and North Carolina to southern Florida and, as far as the Rio Grande, into Texas. He swims up the river which gave him his name to southern Arkansas and Oklahoma. Intensively hunted for his skin for decades, he came within an ace of extinction but has now made a comeback helped by an effective protection program. A natural survivor, the alligator has learned to adapt to the winter droughts that dry up his swamp habitat. When searching for water, he is forced to cross parched bottomland but carefully lifts his long body to travel faster and to leave no tell-tale drag mark. Sooner or later, his obstinacy and his instinct lead him to hollows where the ground water lies just below the surface. Using his powerful tail and his long muzzle, he begins to dig energetically until the water begins to well up. Once settled, he spends the entire winter in these wet hollows, which he clears regularly, until the first rains arrive. By preventing these natural limestone basins from silting up and becoming choked with weeds, he actively contributes to the preservation of this natural environment. The alligator pits, spread throughout the swamp, attract a host of thirsty animal visitors. Fish, molluscs, herons and otters soon move in to

form a microcosm which the master of the house leaves in peace, preferring to live on his reserves of fat and economize all effort. Because of the long list of animals he helps survive the droughts, the rangers in the Everglades National Park have nick-named the alligator 'guardian of the swamps'. When the rains finally return, all the participants in these winter microcosms return to their usual activities, appetites return and the truce is declared over.

Powdered with leaves in the black waters of the Okefenokee Swamp,
these alligators maintain their motionless vigil. Much more common than the rare American
crocodile, they are easily distinguished by their shorter, broader muzzles. Georgia.

Spanish moss drapes these bald cypresses
in North Carolina's Merchants Millpond State Park.

*Strange knobbly knees help bald cypresses
to breathe in an otherwise waterlogged environment.
Atchafalaya Basin, Louisiana.*

EVERGLADES

A PARADISE IN TROUBLED WATERS

One of the first colonists to arrive in southern Florida looked out at the sea of marsh plants growing as far as the eye could see between the fringes of mangroves and named the area after these 'glades' which stretched for 'ever'. This huge marsh, covering some 5,000 square miles today, is in fact one of the world's strangest rivers - a river between forty and sixty miles wide but only six inches deep which used to flow freely down from Lake Okeechobee, its source, to the sea. Moving over a bed of porous limestone sloping three inches to the mile, it moves so slowly that a drop of water from the lake takes years to meet the Gulf of Mexico. Partly liquid, partly vegetation, this flow was named Pa-hay-okee, the river-of-grass, by the Indians. No majestic waterfalls, no red-rock canyons, no

glaciers and no grizzly bears in the Everglades; this second largest of the national parks in the lower 48 offers few of the spectacular attractions the others preserve and many Americans fail to understand its protected status. At first sight, the Everglades seem just a mosquito-infested flat swampland. Yet on closer inspection, visitors begin to appreciate the subtlety and mysterious beauty of these landscapes. On cloudless days the horizon etches a line across a landscape without a frame, a landscape with no volume and no relief, half blue, half green. Drowned in vegetation, the dividing line between land and water is so blurred that only a low-altitude flyover or a canoe trip allow us to appreciate the mosaic of different ecosystems contained in the flow of this pancake-flat marshland. The prairies of saw grass, a 10-foot tall sedge with razor-sharp edges, so stiff that only a cyclone can flatten it, draw their nourishment from an almost immobile sheet of fresh water. Clumps of bald cypresses thrive in hollows where sandy peat accumulates. Little rises, less than three feet high, harbor tropical jungles composed mainly of broad-leaved trees whose roots dislike being submerged. The deep, humus-rich soil of these 'hammocks' welcomes mahoganies, palms, sweet gums and even banyans, whose seeds have been carried over from the West Indies. Some species from the more temperate regions, such as the live oaks, add to the diversity. The Eliott pine and the saw palmetto, immune to the fires which long ravaged the park, cover the low limestone hills like those of Long Pine Key. The southern coastline, where the river water mingles with the saltwater, is the kingdom of the mangrove, a tropical colonizer whose efforts are often destroyed by the hurricanes. Protected by the coral chain of the Florida Keys, the warm, shallow waters of the Florida Bay offer a feast of marine vegetation for a host of living organisms.
In the gloom of the flooded forests, in the sedges which fringe a labyrinth of water

Mangroves colonize the shoreline along the semi-tropical regions of southern Florida. Everglades National Park. Bald cypresses also grow readily in drier environments like this coastal prairie in the Everglades.

channels, on the ground and in the trees, thousands of creatures live to the rhythm of droughts and torrential rains in a tropical hothouse atmosphere. More than 600 kinds of animals, not including the mosquitoes and other uncounted insects, and some 900 plant species make up the bubbling richness of the Everglades park. When established in 1947, the park offered protection to the great egrets and the snowy egrets, threatened by plume hunters, and to many other endangered species such as the snail kite, a rare raptor which preys only on 'ligs', the colorful Florida tree snails so prized by collectors. The slow-breeding American wood stork, the extremely rare American crocodile and the peaceful manatee are also threatened with extinction. While the manatees prefer the bay waters and the marshes, the Florida panther opts for the prairies and pine forests. This big cat is today one of the most threatened animals in North America; the Big Cypress preserve probably harbors fewer than thirty remaining specimens. This natural variety underscores the park's double designation as an international biosphere reserve and a UNESCO world heritage site.

Carpeting the salt marshes with their poor soil,
this savannah dotted with dwarf cypresses contrasts sharply with the generally lusher vegetation ▷
elsewhere in the Everglades National Park. Florida.

In the middle of the Caribbean,
the Virgin Islands National Park protects an astonishing wealth of undersea ecosystems
which include the delicate coral reefs and the grazing grounds for sea turtles.

HURRICANES: DESTROYERS AND BENEFACTORS

The Everglades park lies in the path of the hurricanes which strike this region of Florida regularly, causing immense damage both to the natural environment and to human infrastructures. One of the most devastating in a century, Hurricane Andrew, lashed the coast with winds of over 200 miles an hour in 1992. Yet even at these speeds, it's an ill wind that blows nobody any good and Andrew had beneficial results on certain parts of the ecosystem. Where thousands of trees were blown over like straw and others had their tops stripped off, space was cleared for new life to develop. Many plant species immediately colonized these new niches where the tree screen had hitherto prevented light from filtering down to the forest floor.

The sub-tropical climate encourages lush vegetation on all levels,
sprouting from the ground, springing from the swamps or clinging to the branches of a host
like this bay tree in Florida's Big Cypress Preserve.

THE EMPIRE OF THE EVERGLADES

A roseate spoonbill probing the muddy waters with its curious beak or a long flight of pelicans against a ruby-red sky: sights which delight lovers of an apparently-intact nature. Yet the natural riches of the park have been slowly but inexorably draining away for many years now. In the early days of the 20th century, politicians promised to build the 'Empire of the Everglades'. Canals were dug, levees were raised and the river flow diverted and controlled. Everything was done to irrigate the ripe agricultural land and supply the water requirements of the millions of migrants to southern Florida. Over 1400 miles of canals and dikes now criss-cross the region, constricting the top three-quarters of the river into a concrete straitjacket. More than 50% of the wet zones have disappeared, destroying the ecosystems, aggravating the droughts and severely affecting the bird populations. This upstate destruction of the swamplands has had a ripple effect on Florida Bay. Once famed for its crystal waters, it has become opaque and muddy, like milk chocolate, the first sign

Alternating droughts and floods
have determined the distribution and ecological development of the different species
in Florida's most famous park, the Everglades.

of damage to the marine environment. Trail your hand in the water and you can't even see your fingers. Dead sponges and fish now float on the surface. The national park and its surrounding land have reached such a critical state that an ambitious new project has been launched to restore the original natural water flow. The White House has sanctioned this project, a governmental first for a project of this size, further stating that the sugar industry, bitterly opposed to the project, would have to participate financially according to the principle of 'polluter-payer'. *"Tranquil and sure of its serene beauty, this land is not a water distributor but the last beneficiary of waters arriving from elsewhere"*. One of the most daring ecological repair missions in history may well update President Harry Truman's speech when he dedicated the Everglades park back in 1947.

2

THE CENTRAL PLAINS

The prairie, and the Great Lakes

*"To make a prairie it takes a clover
and one bee,
One clover, and a bee,
And revery,
The revery alone will do
If bees are few."*

*Emily Dickinson,
American poetess (1830-1886)*

◁ *Beneath the shortgrass prairie covering
Nebraska's Agate Fossil Beds lie fossilized skeletons of the mammals
which once enjoyed this unlimited grazing.*

Despite their initially uniform appearance, the Great Plains
are in fact a mosaic of separate ecosystems, differing considerably from one another as the seasons change.
Agate Fossil Beds National Monument, Nebraska.

Once past the dense Nordic forest which turns purple and gold in the fall, past the dark lakes where the French-Canadian trappers once hunted the beaver, the moose, the wolf and the grizzly, the heart of the continent stretches from the Appalachians to the Rockies. An endless plain which sapped the spirits of the pioneers with its sheer distance. In The Prairie (1827), James Fenimore Cooper's hero, Natty Bumppo the Leather-Stocking, sets out for the West like so many others and compares the great plains to an ocean, "From time to time in the distance, a great tree emerged from the hollow of the valleys, spreading its withered branches skywards like some solitary vessel. We were driven to the unpalatable conclusion that a very long stretch of country had to be crossed, plains which appeared interminable, before the hopes of a humble farmer might materialize.". *Half a century was all that it took to transform the virgin soil of the central plains forever. The rippling sea of grass gave way to stiff wheatstems, herds of cattle replaced the buffalo and gigantic irrigation networks watered a land once known as the great desert. A rigid grid of irrigation channels and highways now frames the chessboard of fields and crops, leaving little space for the rare ribbons of alluvial forest or still-wild pasture land. These oases of green are living memories of a bygone time when the landscape was only prairie, wind and sky.*

North of the Great Prairie lies a land of water, the region of the Great Lakes.
Apostle Islands National Lakeshore, Lake Superior, Wisconsin.

As their wagons rolled west, the pioneers must have scanned
these horizons in the hope of distinguishing a mountain, a lake or even a tree.
South Pass, Oregon Trail, Wyoming.

Sunrise paints the sky and the calm waters of Lake Superior.
Isle Royale National Park.

LAND OF 10,000 LAKES

'The land of 10,000 lakes', the state nickname of Minnesota, but also appropriate to the entire northeastern part of the United States. The region of the Great Lakes constitutes the world's greatest reserve of freshwater, an aquatic area which plays a key role both on the climate and the economic life of the region. Without counting the myriad smaller lakes which dot the landscape down to the meeting of the Missouri and the Mississippi, Lakes Superior, Michigan, Huron, Erie and Ontario alone cover over 95,000 square miles, more than the entire surface area of Great Britain and Northern Ireland. Their beds were gouged by Quaternary glaciers which flowed down from the Canadian shield, scouring and refashioning the region like giant graders. Around them, a thick layer of glacial deposits nourishes a magnificent, dense forest of now mainly deciduous trees; the white pines have almost all fallen to the loggers' chain saws. Running unbroken for 1500 miles from the shores of New England to the Great Plains, these woods seem a uniform green carpet until the fall arrives and the beeches and sugar maples burst into a festival of color. Away from the big industrial centers, the Lakes region has managed to keep secret pockets of its dense original wilderness hidden away for future generations.

Dancing reflections of pale birch boles in the waters of the world's largest lake.
Isle Royale National Park, Michigan.

Voyageurs, Isle Royale, Grand Portage... the north still carries the imprint of the French-Canadians who developed the fur trade in the 19th century. Voyageurs National Park protects the marshes, the lakes and the deep forests, the same landscape as the traplines those trappers traveled in their birch-bark canoes. Capable of paddling sixteen hours at a stretch along these waterways, they brought back

the Indians, who exploited its copper reserves, before becoming a fishing center in the 19th century. Although its landscapes have changed little since that era, the wildlife population is no longer the same. Wolves arrived in 1948, padding across the ice bridge over from Canada to settle comfortably in their new domain. Their presence has reestablished the balance between predator and

their feather-light craft laden low with furs. Today's visitors still visit the park on foot or by canoe. The beavers, as landscape architects, are extremely important to the park's ecosystems. By building their dams, they slow the water flow and allow aquatic plants to develop, thereby providing food for the fish and insects which are in turn consumed by the birds and bears.

Isle Royale, on Lake Superior, is really an archipelago of wooded islands, clear lakes and green shorelines. Only accessible by boat and thus naturally protected, it forms a living laboratory. Granted national park status in 1931, it was upgraded to a biosphere in 1980. The Isle was long inhabited by

prey, eliminating the former overpopulation of moose.

Around a headland, behind a grove of maples... the lakeside landscapes are full of surprises. We suddenly run out of vegetation and into sandy beaches protected by the bulk of the Sleeping Bear dunes or the Indiana dunes. Coastal currents have collected glacial deposits which the wind moves at will, depositing them on the slopes of the high dunes. Towards the south and west, the wooded landscape stops abruptly, cut short by the drier climate and the lumbermen, giving way to one of the world's great grain-crop regions. This was where the prairie began.

Irises, water lilies and snake grass carpet the many lakes in Minnesota's Voyageurs National Park.

Accessible only by air or water,
Isle Royale has remained an archipelago
of unspoiled beauty.
The colored cliffs of Pictured Rocks National
Lakeshore supply beaches with multicolored stones
polished by the cold waves of Lake Superior.
Unaffected by the chill water, moose wade in to browse
on the aquatic plants. Michigan.

The Dakota Indians called Minnesota the 'sky-tinted water',
a name that could be applied to all the region of the Great Lakes.
Tahguamenon River, Michigan.

Before joining the Missouri,
the Niobrara River meanders peacefully through magnificent expanses of tallgrass prairie.
Agate Fossil Beds National Monument, Nebraska

FOSSILS UNDER THE PRAIRIE

This immense prairie used to cover, a long time ago, over one and a half million square miles of plains from Canada down to Texas. A unique environment occupying a quarter of the United States, the life support for 60 to 70 million buffalo, almost as many pronghorn, millions of deer, wolves and grizzlies, not to mention the prairie dogs and a whole microcosm of living creatures. An ecosystem so extended that it has been labeled 'the characteristic landscape of North America'. The roots of the prairie sink into the geological history of this central basin. The story begins some 75 million years ago, at the time when a shallow sea covered the plains. During the intense seismic phase which gave birth to the Rockies, the seabed found itself uncovered. This last layer of the ancient sea is seen in a layer of grayish sediments containing an incredible diversity of fossilized marine creatures - mollusks, crabs, sea-snails, squids, cuttlefish, octopuses... The warm, damp climate favored the development of a lush sub-tropical forest which lasted for millions of years. When the climate grew colder again, the forest first thinned to savanna and then to prairie. The emergence of the Rockies and the Black Hills was completed by another volcanic phase which came to a peak some 35 million years ago. A thick layer of ash fell over the prairie, sealing the marine deposits. Many fossils have been found in this ash, including the bones of the great mammals which roamed the region, the camel, the saber-toothed cat and an ancestor of the rhinoceros, the *Metamynodon.* Herds of a gazelle-camel, the six-foot *Stenomylus,* galloped next to *Menoceras,* a pony-sized rhinoceros over the Agate Fossil Beds in Nebraska. Through paleontological discoveries made in other national monuments such as Wyoming's Fossil Butte, Idaho's Hagerman Fossil Beds or Colorado's Florissant Fossil Beds, scientists have been able to study the interrelations between plants and animals of the Cenozoic era and record the climatic variations which have followed one another down through the past 65 million years until the growth of the modern prairie.

*Herds of pronghorns and wild mustangs
still roam the shrinking tracts of the Great Prairies.*

*The Devil's Tower, an imposing 600-foot shaft of volcanic rock
towering 1300 feet above the Belle Fourche River,
was the first of America's National Monuments, established in 1906.*

THE ROOTS OF THE SKY

Away in the distance, earth and sky meet to share the horizon. The view stretches over an infinite landscape of rolling hills, a landscape in constant movement, tousled by the wind. Freedom and solitude are our trail companions. Long or short, the waving prairie grass paints the sky and, beneath the sod, sinks deep roots to capture the water it needs. Mown, cropped, trampled or burned, the grass always springs back with renewed energy drawn from those long roots which carefully absorb and store the slightest drop of moisture. The continental climate reigns over central plains, characterized by extreme thermal amplitudes. In the hydric shadow of the Rockies and the Appalachians, they receive little rainfall, neither from the west nor the east, but are constantly swept by the winds. A warm, damp wind blows up from the Gulf of Mexico in the summer and the cold, dry chinook sweeps down from Canada in the winter, increasing from time to time to freezing blizzard. The different faces of the plains depend on the quantity of rain they receive. The shortgrass prairie covers the drier soils, near the foot of the Rockies, where the buffalo grass and other short-stemmed pasture grasses form a thin steppe. The tallgrass prairie grows over to the east, as far from the mountains as possible, where it benefits from the damp Gulf Stream air currents. Between the two, in the middle portion of the

Great Plains, the mixed prairie is a mosaic of tall grass, cropped grazing pasture and calf-high meadow grasses. Wind Cave National Park, in South Dakota, is a magnificent example of these prairie landscapes. The grass growth also depends on the nature of the soil and on the prairie fires. In the absence of natural fires, whenever the climate cools and the rains increase, trees invade the high plains and gradually screen off this open environment. If, on the contrary, the rains diminish and the temperatures rise, the south-western deserts begin to nibble the prairie. Fire is thus essential for the survival of these grasslands. The Indians used to fertilize and rejuvenate the plains by lighting fires which swept across the dry grasses with the speed of a 'red buffalo'. The soul of the prairie can be captured in the silky swish of nodding heads of grass, flaxen as Norsemen, rising and bending under the hand of the wind, in the dainty form of a pronghorn skirting the dunes at sunset in search of drinking water, the hair on its rump all a-quiver, ready to rise at the slightest hint of danger. The white underhair stands out like a flashing warning light for all others in the herd. The Theodore Roosevelt National Park in North Dakota, created in 1978, protects the wild mustangs which have now been recognized as part of North America's cultural heritage.

*As winter approaches,
the bitter Chinook wind sweeps down from Canada to frost this tallgrass prairie preserve in Bazaar, Kansas.*

*The clay and sandstone cliffs along the horizon in these Nebraskan grasslands
are gradually but inexorably worn down by the combined action of wind and water erosion.
Oglala National Grasslands & Scotts Bluff National Monument.*

COLORS OF THE PRAIRIE

The prairie grasses come in shades of pastel, like a watercolor painted in ochers and pale yellows, in verdigris and in bluish tints rather than bold splashes. They have no need to stand out, no need to attract the eye, because they have no need to tempt insects to be pollinated. The omnipresent wind takes charge of dispersing their pollen across the land. Although, in sheer vegetal mass, the prairie constitutes a sea of grass, almost three plants out of four are wildflowers. In the shade of the tall grasses, they form a lilliputian jungle whose inhabitants take their turn in flowering as the seasons change. The first blooms appear in late

March, the bright colors of the anemones and the crowfoot standing out vividly against the prairie's ash-colored winter mantle. In late April the buttercups, Maximilian's sunflowers, sagebrush and mints burst into bloom. The stiff goldenrod and the smooth asters on their fragile stems await full summer before blossoming. In September, when the prairie begins to yellow, the primroses, gentians, sunflowers and asters continue their parade. A carpet of flowers, the prairie becomes the promised land for the butterflies. Now that the ecosystem of the land has been broken up by agriculture, many of the wildflowers have disappeared or become so scarce that only the trained eye of a botanist can spot them. This is the case for the wild orchids and the echinacea or purple coneflower, a coarse little herb with purple flowers which the medicine men of the Plains Indians used to heal so many ailments, from a simple cold to a snakebite.

This natural landmark, filed down by erosion,
is now a national historic site in memory of the pioneers who broke their journey west
at its base. Chimney Rock, Nebraska.

Spring rainfall triggers a summer-long flowering of prairie plants but in other seasons,
combed by desiccating winds, the plains become a sea of brittle blond grass.
Oglala National Grasslands, Nebraska.

THE END OF THE BUFFALO GOD

Traveling through the tall prairie grass in the 1830s, Captain Bonneville reined up on a butte, astonished to discover *"as far as the eye could see, a land completely black with herds"*. Similarly, in 1837, one of the steamboats paddling up the Mississippi had to suddenly stop all machines and wait hours while one of the herds swam the river. When the Europeans first began to encroach on the land, the buffalo population has been estimated at around 65 million. For the Plains Indians, the buffalo was and always had been an inexhaustible resource. They used his hides for their clothes, their moccasins and their tepees, his meat to feed them... and indeed organized their whole lives and nomadic wanderings around him. Indian mythology associated the buffalo with the God of nourishment, of fecundation, of power and of courage. The Sioux chief Black Elk recounted the dramatic destiny of this animal venerated as a divinity, *"the white man didn't kill them for food; he killed them in exchange for guns. He only kept the skins to sell. I've heard tell of boats going down the Missouri loaded with dried buffalo tongues. Sometimes, even, he took nothing, just killing them for pleasure."*. When the beaver populations were on the brink of extinction, the fur companies demanded buffalo robes. And, from the 1830s onwards, a policy of systematic extermination was applied to the buffalo in the aim of depriving the Indians of their main source of existence. When the first railroad spanned the continent in 1869, the curtain went up on a carnage. Millions of animals were slaughtered to feed the construction workmen. A certain William Frederick Cody was hired as a meat supplier by the railroad and gained dubious fame and the nickname 'Buffalo Bill' by providing 4,280 carcasses (by his own count) in seventeen months. Much more repugnant were the hunting parties which developed later. Leaning out of carriage windows, railroad travellers shot at the fleeing herds. The carcasses, left intact and bleeding, piled up on either side of the rails. Of the four subspecies of the American bison, two were wiped out completely. The Eastern buffalo disappeared in 1825, followed by the Oregon buffalo in 1850. The wood buffalo is the only ancient race still surviving in a small herd near the Great Slave Lake. By 1875, the last survivors of the endless herds were estimated at 500, scattered among zoos and private ranches.

In the 1830s, before the 'sportsmen' organized
shooting parties from the comfort of railroad cars, the first explorers of the Great Plains
found a land 'completely darkened' by the passing buffalo herds.

THE ETERNAL NOMAD OF THE PRAIRIES

With heads kept lowered, their eyes so black that they disappear into the thick curly mane, the buffaloes keep moving. Just one step at a time, two at the most, their hooves crunching through the frozen snow and their breath steaming in the chill morning air, mingling with the mist floating above the river. A few minutes before sunrise, the rime still powders their muzzles, their massive heads and their humped backs. They don't seem to mind the freezing temperatures. Even when the thermometer plummets to -30°C, they still wander across the plains in search of the scanty pasture covered by three feet of snow. The cows and calves are a little farther off, away from the adult males. They all go their own ways, in little groups. The buffalo are always on the move at dawn, looking for new grazing and eating at

intervals. Later in the day, generally in the afternoon, they lie in the shade and chew their cud for long periods. In winter the days are too short and they often continue feeding at night by the light of the moon. All through the day, they continue moving together in the same direction. Grazing, like rumination, is a business where imitation plays an important role; each animal watches the others and follows their example, stimulated in his own activity by his observation of his companions. This is what scientists call allelomimetic behavior. This heavy feeder, with a daily intake of over 50 pounds of nourishment, cannot stay long in the same place. After ten to fifteen days in one area, they set off in search of fresh pastures in their endless grazing cycle. Difficult to know whether they move randomly, or whether they are guided by some inbuilt navigation system or even some search for new flavors in the pastureland. The taste and the texture of their grazing does play an important role in their choice of food, fleshy plants being their favorites. Having no upper incisors, the buffalo wraps his tongue round a clump of vegetation and cuts a mouthful free with his lower incisors. By chewing his cud later, he is able to extract the maximum of energy from a diet low on protein and rich in fiber. Powerful jaw muscles allow him to chew roots and to open his mouth wide enough to strip bark from the trees.

Despite their imposing bulk and generally slow-moving behavior, buffaloes are surprisingly agile. Threatened by danger, they break into a gallop and can exceed 38 miles an hour. When running flat out, the animal's enormous weight is carried on one or two legs at the most. His body remains bunched and his hooves seem to barely skim the ground. Protected by the national parks and increasingly ranched for beef, the North American buffalo population now comfortably exceeds 200,000. The largest wild herds are to be found in Yellowstone, Wind Cave, Montana's National Bison Range and the Badlands National Park

*In summer as in winter, the buffalo spend their days wandering over the prairie,
whether grazing in hock-deep snows or impassively chewing their cud in the heat of summer.
Yellowstone National Park, Wyoming.*

BADLANDS

Cool and refreshing, dusk falls on the Badlands. Outsize shadows stretch towards an ink-blue sky as the sun slowly slips below the horizon. In the horizontal light, the landscape stands up like a stage setting. The last rays catch the highest buttes for an instant and they shine like gold. The wind dies down, soothed by nightfall, and new sounds come out of the gathering darkness. The meadowlarks trill their evening song above the murmur of the Little Missouri river. The hooves of the bison and the deer click monotonically over

the hard clay. The mustangs shake their manes against the disappearing sky. The Badlands are alive. Situated in the south-western part of South Dakota, they cover over 50,000 square miles. The combined action of water and freezing ravaged these Tertiary table-lands, leaving a fantastic - almost lunar - landscape of pinnacles, peaks, buttes and ravines, all delicately colored.

Men have looked at these badlands for centuries with a mixture of fear and fascination. Well before the French-Canadian trappers, unable to lay down trails, called this region the 'bad lands to cross', the Lakota Indians had already come to the same conclusion, naming it 'Maka Sicha', the bad lands. The Badlands are a place of extremes, fried by heat and the violence of electrical storms in summer and frozen by blizzards in winter. The naked reliefs erode whenever water courses through the canyons. The White river carries away over an inch of sediments every year. A place of extremes, but also of beauty. A spare beauty revealed by the full moon illuminating a landscape on the borders of creation and decadence. The alternate layers of crumbly sediments, colored markers of former seas, and of volcanic ash add interest and movement to this beauty. The eye follows each layer of color from one butte to another, one pinnacle to the next, one side to the other of the ravines. Seen from the air, they become the lines on a topographical map, tracing the geological history of the region.

*The moon slowly rises over the Badlands,
barring the course of the Missouri on its way across Montana. Missouri River Breaks.*

*These aptly-named Badlands are clay plateaux, scoured and ravaged by the combined action
of frost and erosion. Badlands National Park, South Dakota.*

FROM MALEDICTION TO PROTECTION

While geologists and paleontologists explain the Badlands as a product of terrestrial forces, speaking in measured scientific terms of ancient seas, of temperature changes and of primeval rivers, the Sioux story-tellers recount the malediction which fell on their

lands. They speak of a fertile plain, covered with bison grazing on the thick grass, of a place of harmony where, every fall, the tribes hunted, gathered the wild harvest and met in peaceful council. Yet this Eden was not eternal. Trouble came from the west in the form of a savage tribe, moving down from their mountains. Unable to resist, the Plains Indians called on the Great Spirit to help them. The land suddenly trembled with a rumbling. The sky grew black and was rent with lightning. Fire broke out, all around, and the earth became a sea of flames. Then, just as suddenly, the terror ceased and the sky cleared. The enemy was destroyed but the land remained a disaster and the Badlands were born. Written in blood, the date of December 28th 1890 reminds us that the malediction fell a second time on the Indian lands. Over 150 Indian men, women and children were executed at Wounded Knee, near Pine Ridge near the Nebraskan state line south of the Badlands park, following the prohibition of a Spirit Dance, and the proud Sioux territory became a reserve. Part of the region was classified a National Monument in 1939 to safe-guard its rich ecological, geological and cultural heritage. With the agreement of its residents, the Pine Ridge Indian reserve was later protected and the Badlands National Park was finally created in 1978.

Alternating layers of crumbly sediment,
color-coded reminders of vanished seas, lead the eye across the ravines from one outcrop to the next.
Badlands National Park, South Dakota & Theodore Roosevelt National Park, North Dakota.

These barren clay landscapes, inhospitable in the extreme and unsuited for any agriculture,
◁ *have always inspired mixed feelings of fear and fascination.*
Toadstool Area, Oglala National Grasslands, Nebraska.

These strange landscapes are a region of extremes,
branded by flickering lightning storms during the summer heat and scoured by bitter winds in the winter.
Badlands National Park, South Dakota.

The black-footed ferret, thought extinct since 1979,
has now reappeared in its natural habitat, the prairie.

MEANWHILE, BACK HOME ON THE RANGE ...

In 1981, the scientific community was rocked with a most exciting discovery. A black-footed ferret *(Mustela nigripes)*, considered extinct since the death of the last captive specimen in 1979, had been rediscovered, alive and well, on the plains of Wyoming. The news was encouraging but not necessarily a guarantee of survival for this little nocturnal hunter with the bandit mask. Dependent on the prairie ecosystem, its natural habitat and, especially, on the prairie dog populations, the black-footed ferret remains North America's rarest mammal. The constant division of the plains, the systematic destruction of the prairie dog towns and a wave of epidemics almost destroyed the ferret colony a few years after its discovery, cutting their number to only eighteen. Braving criticism, the biologists of the Game and Fish Department took the risk of capturing these survivors and attempting to start a captive breeding program. The gamble paid off and thirty-six ferrets were released into the Badlands National Park during the fall of 1994. Litters have since been born on the park's prairies and the black-footed ferret, like the buffalo, once again occupies its place in the natural ecosystem of the Great Plains.

3

THE ROCKY MOUNTAINS

The myth of the frontier

"Nature has fixed the limits of our nation;
charitably, she has marked our western frontier with almost
inaccessible mountains whose base is ringed
by sterile sandy deserts".

F.J. Turner,
American historian (1861-1932)

Sprague Lake, in the Rocky Mountain National Park,
◁ *mirrors an early morning sky and the wavy peaks of the surrounding mountains.*
The Rockies contain many of these lakes gouged out by the ancient glaciers. Colorado.

The awe-inspiring barrier of the Rockies long remained an impossible obstacle for the pioneers.
Pushed up by the grinding encounter of two tectonic plates, the Rockies run like a giant wall from north to south.
Grand Teton National Park, Wyoming.

In one single sentence, Frederick Jackson Turner, the creator of the frontier myth, summed up the character and symbolic importance of the Rocky Mountains. Prior to the Louisiana Purchase, whereby Napoleon sold territory stretching from the Mississippi to the Rockies to the United States for $15 million, the existence of such a wild and grandiose region somewhere in the west was scarcely imagined. The United States doubled its domain with the addition of these 828,000 square miles, acquired for less than 3 cents an acre, and it was now time to explore this new acquisition. Thus, in 1803, President Jefferson entrusted his private secretary, Captain Meriwether Lewis, and William Clark with the task. By discovering the barrier of the Rockies and, especially, by surmounting it, the explorers pushed back the 'last frontier' to the shores of the Pacific. Yet with their imposing bulk, the Rocky Mountains still disdainfully barred the way for generations of daring adventurers and all but the bravest pioneers. Originally known as the 'Stony Mountains', the Rockies live up to their name, composed as they are of densely-packed hard rock. With many peaks over 10,000 feet[3] , they have become the roof of North America, a double-sloping roof with its ridgepole forming a watershed north-south from Alaska down to Mexico and running through six of the contiguous United States (Montana, Idaho, Wyoming, Colorado, Utah and Nevada). The Continental Divide of America separates the continent between two oceans.

Sunset over Island Lake in the Bridger Wilderness. Wind River Range, Wyoming.

[3] over 100 in the Rocky Mountain National Park alone

Century plants seem to rise to meet the dawn in Big Bend National Park, Texas, a region known as despoblado, a Spanish term meaning 'the empty country'.

BIRTH OF A MOUNTAIN

It is undoubtedly from the crest line, over 12,000 feet above sea level where the wind clears the air, that the Rocky Mountains are most beautiful. A petrified ocean seems to open beneath the mountaineer's feet; crests of ice, snowy spume, waves of stone, escarpments, needles, canyons, rock falls and walls like breakwaters extend to the far horizon. From up here, the Rockies seem younger and somehow more real. Seen from the Great Plains, the mountain wall towers solid and massive. Looking at these monolithic forms with their flattened summits, only a specialist can distinguish the history of a

geological upheaval. The first signs of the Rockies' emergence from the Pacific cordillera date back to some 170 million years ago. While the development of the Atlantic ocean was pushing the American continent away from Europe, the Farallon tectonic plate, much harder, crushed up against the west coast of America. The collision was so violent and the forces so powerful that the shock wave ran inland and crumpled the earth's crust into what might be called the 'first Rockies'. All the geological episodes involved in the creation of the mountain chain can be seen in the Glacier, Grand Teton and

cont. page 156

Pitiless winter blasts these summits of rock and ice for practically six months a year.
Rocky Mountains National Park, Colorado.
Away in the distance, the peaks of the Rockies form the spine of America,
the continental divide from Alaska to Mexico.

Mount Clements Glacier N.P., Montana.

*Beaten and toughened by the rigors of the climate, lashed by wind, rain and snow, the roots of
this whitebark pine have become practically indistinguishable from the rocks that gave these mountains their name.
Wind River Range, Wyoming & Glacier National Park, Montana.*

All the geological episodes in the creation of the Rockies
can be read in the landscapes of the national parks which protect the chain.
Boulder field in Horseshoe Park, Colorado, and sedimentary rock in Montana's Glacier Park.

The mineral shores of St Mary Lake. Right on the Canadian border,
Glacier National Park offers geologists the possibility of studying very ancient and remarkably
well preserved rock formations. Montana.

The rigorous climate and abrupt slopes of the Rockies offer vegetation few opportunities.
Only lichens and occasional alpines such as these greenleaf bluebells manage to gain toeholds in the granite walls.
Rocky Mountain National Park, Colorado.

Rocky Mountain national parks. Like uncut books, they have protected the virgin pages of these unspoiled zones and lofty summits.

Spreading up to the Canadian border, Glacier National Park allows us to admire the most ancient and certainly the best preserved geological formations. The slopes of the park are built up of a succession of marine sediments deposited between two billion and 800,000,000 years ago when the seas had flooded the region. Visitors can enjoy the curious experience of feeling, at 9000 feet above sea level, the traces left imprinted in the rock by the lapping waves of the Primary era, the cracks left in the Precambrian dried mud and the marks of water droplets left on what was the seabed at that time. Some seventy million years ago, violent tectonic shocks lifted a layer, hundreds of meters thick, of these sedimentary rocks, cracking it and sending gigantic blocks hurtling for miles on either side of the fault line. These blocks, blown out from deep below, explain why the ancient seabeds are now at 9000 feet. The strange monolith of Chief Mountain, a solitary stone statue on the eastern borders of the park, is an eloquent reminder of these telluric forces.

*Lichens spread unaffected by the harsh climate on the limestone walls
and the metamorphic rocks of Glacier National Park, Montana.*

During the Cretaceous period, somewhere between the Mesozoic (or Secondary) and the Tertiary eras, another orogenic phase produced new fault breaks and overlaps which thrust up the Laramie Range in Wyoming and pushed the mountains a little higher to the 14,000 foot peaks we see today. The heat from within the earth's crust burst to the surface in intense volcanic activity which created the Absaroka range and gave birth to the geysers, fumaroles and sulfur springs in the Yellowstone region. Between phases of relative calm, the Rockies were again shaken by seismic forces towards the end of the Tertiary era. Huge eruptions of lava spilled down into the valleys, creating the Columbia plateaux in the north towards today's Canada, and a final tectonic thrust created the Grand Tetons. A gigantic vertical shearing action, in some places over almost 30,000 feet, perched beds of pink limestone on the summit of Mount Moran, at around 6000 feet above Jackson Hole, and buried the same beds some 20,000 feet below the surface of the valley. All along this mountain spine, despite the successive upheavals of the land around them, the rivers have continued to dig ever-deepening canyons. The national parks which enclose these landscapes today, criss-crossed with trails and hiking paths, have become open-air workshops for geologists from all over the world.

Lake Solitude in the heart of Wyoming's Grand Teton Park.
Spring skies may have arrived, but the lakes of this region keep their mantle of ice
for more than six months of the year.

This spectacular monolith, looming over the prairie,
is a vestige of the tectonic and erosive forces which shaped the Rockies.
Chief Mountain, Glacier National Park, Montana.

160

*The Rockies become mountains of light and color
when the clear mountain streams reveal their mosaic beds and the wildflowers carpet the alpine meadows.
Glacier National Park, Montana.*

While fog veils the base of the Tetons,
irises find rich nourishment in the glacier deposits known as moraines
in Colorado's Rocky Mountain National Park.

*Summer snowmelt powers this mountain stream cascading
down the slopes of Glacier National Park, Montana.*

ETERNAL YOUTH

Fashioned and re-fashioned by the seismic and volcanic activity which still shakes the West, and especially by the continued glacial erosion, the slopes and peaks explored by today's backpackers and mountaineers have been kept eternally young. Glacier. The name of this famous park was not chosen for the tiny glaciers which still cling to its highest summits. No indeed, it refers back to the morphological inheritance left by the Quaternary ice age, by the thick layer of ice which, for the last

two or three million years, covered the Glacier region and the whole chain of the Rockies. The glaciers crept down the canyons of the time, plowing and grading the landscape and pushing all the resulting debris in front of them. Water trickled into the tiniest fissures of the rock, froze and cracked it wide open. The accumulation of snow and ice gouged out increasingly perfect cirques. When the great thaw finally came, the glaciers left a series of pointed crests, as sharp as

*The turquoise waters of one of the innumerable lakes
left by the ice ages in Glacier National Park and its sister park, Waterton Lakes, across the Canadian border.*

Marmots leave their winter dens to enjoy the spring sunshine atop the San Juan Mountains in Colorado.

*The rich diversity of vegetation from the stony summits
down the alpine meadows to the grassy valleys attracts a correspondingly rich diversity of wildlife.
Large herbivores such as elk, moose and the Rocky Mountain bighorn sheep abound.
Yellowstone and Grand Teton National Parks, Wyoming.*

the 'Garden Wall', like a stone lacework of ice-polished rock, and a multitude of lakes. Lakes Avalanche, Iceberg and Gunsight are all glacial in origin. Indeed, the park owes more than its name to the glaciers. With some 200 lakes, miles of mountain torrents and brilliantly-hued forests, the outstanding beauty of this glacial park has long

of wild animal life. Trout enjoy the meltwaters of glacial lakes. Flat valley bottoms, dotted here and there with stands of poplar, aspen and conifers, are favorite spots for buffalo, mule deer, white-tailed deer and rutting stags during the fall. Beaver, moose, coyotes, swans and bald eagles prefer the peaceful oxbows of the Snake River

been recognized and protected. In 1910, it was set aside as a national park. Twenty-two years later, in 1932, the Canadian and United States governments joined forces to create the first 'international peace park' by twinning Glacier with Waterton Lake across the border, thereby announcing that protection of the environment does not stop at national frontiers. In 1995, this double park, its remarkable biological diversity underlined by the presence of major carnivores such as wolves, grizzly bears and cougars, finally became a world heritage site. Geological history determines vegetation which, in turn, governs the abundance and distribution

in its unhurried progress through the Jackson Hole valley.
Bighorn sheep and mountain goats, living symbols of the Rockies, are the unquestioned masters of the high peaks. A former miner's tenacity and love of nature were behind the creation of Rocky Mountain national park in 1915. Enos Mills struggled for six years, battling trappers, hunters and the forest authorities to have this land set aside, over a quarter of a million acres which protect the flora and fauna at all altitudes from the plains to the high tundra above the timberline which covers more than a third of its surface.

Coursing down from the glaciers and the snow fields, water is omnipresent in Glacier National Park.
Using patience and time, it carves the rocks, hollowing, honing and polishing them.

*At the southern end of the Rockies, the Rio Grande has worn a passage through a succession of sierras,
isolating buttes and carving deep canyons. Sierra de Carmen, Big Bend National Park, Texas.*

*Perilously poised, Balanced Rock has lain like this for thousands of years
in the Grapevine Hills of Big Bend National Park.*

THE ROCKY MOUNTAINS' OWN GOAT

Smooth and sparkling, the schist rock wall is blurred by the first flurry of snow. Unmindful of the worsening weather or of the giddy drop below, a white form wafts across the crystalline cliff face. A solitary mountain goat continues his way down, pausing a little farther along on the brink of a cleft in the rock. After a mere second of hesitation, the goat springs out into space and disappears. Is it the falling snow or did he miss his footing? Suddenly he reappears, some fifteen feet down the face. Another ten feet and we catch another glimpse of the ghostly form, trotting towards

a tuft of grass spared by the frost. These fleeting pictures are only too seldom shared by the visitors to the Glacier national park because this natural acrobat has chosen to live in the austere realm of ice and rock at the very summit of the Rockies. Oreamnos americanus, the Rocky Mountain goat, is found only in North America, and most notably in the mountain regions from south-eastern Alaska down to the center of Idaho and west to Montana. Totally protected by law, the mountain goat is still very sensitive to human disturbances such as road-building, development of tourist areas or the chain saws of the lumbermen. Measures have been taken to increase its numbers, including recent reintroduction programs in Colorado and South Dakota, and the overall population is reckoned at 100,000, spread over the alpine and sub-alpine regions of North America. Up there, on these knife edges between the sky and the snow, the mountain goat reigns over the difficult terrain beyond the timberline. In winter, when this wasteland of rock and ice lies exposed to subzero temperatures, abandoned by all other animals, the mountain goat has no real enemies. Each detail of its anatomy points to its marvelous adaptation to the cold and to its mountain environment. Its artiodactyl hooves allow it to move as surely on vertical rock as on ice and its relatively short legs, powerfully muscled, give it the deliberate gait of the experienced mountaineer, a gait which belies its outstanding agility. Its long, narrow body is made for hugging the rock walls as it travels along tiny ledges. Its long white hair and wooly underfur insulate it from the cold and allow it to blend into the surrounding snow if threatened by daring predators such as the mountain lion or bald eagle. In the last century, this coat was highly appreciated by spinners, who considered it finer than the famous cashmere, and almost led to the extinction of its owner. In the spring, the goats move down into the prairies to gorge on the wild flowers and to replenish their stocks of the mineral salts essential to their metabolism. This need leads them to travel miles to scrape and lick the layers of clay in the road embankments, thereby offering park tourists a rare view of this unrivaled mountaineer.

The mule deer wander everywhere
across the Rockies, from the lush valley floors to the boulder-strewn highlands.
Bears are also great wanderers, but less commonly seen.

EACH TO HIS OWN ALTITUDE

When the mud on the trails, frozen throughout the winter, begins to melt, the message is clear; spring is on the way. Here in the west, spring is a season as short as the goose days of the fall. In April, when a thick mantle of snow still blankets the high prairies, the chipmunk comes out to enjoy a sun-bath after seven months of hibernation. In early May the aspens green. Later, towards July, when the woods ring with the blue jay's cackle, winter relinquishes his cold grip on the land definitively. If the thermometer rises sufficiently, the high prairies are in turn blanketed with wild flowers. They last only a few weeks but their profusion feeds the nesting birds and allows the grizzly to browse

With its short, powerfully muscled legs, the Rocky Mountain goat is the undisputed master of the steep, slippery slopes along the treeline and the narrow ledges along the rocky summits.

happily on the slopes of Glacier park. Six weeks at the most to grow, flower, pollinate and sow seed..., plants and animals alike have little time to ensure their survival before the arrival of the winter.

The Rocky mountains stop the clouds which form over the Pacific. The abundant rainfall and cool, damp climate generate the growth of heavy forest on the western slopes. This rainfall, combined with altitude, determines the type of vegetation. Up to around 300 feet, the predominance of yellow pine (such as the ponderosa) indicates a first zone. Upwards, to around 6000 feet, the straight pine gives way to a gnarled variety which, despite appearances, can grow to some 75 feet. According to the different soil types, these pines are mixed with tamaracks, evergreen Douglas firs or red cedars. Beyond 6000 feet, only the subalpine firs and larches can resist the rigors of the climate.

THE FLUTTERING ASPEN

The Rocky mountains' most emblematic tree is not a somber Douglas or one of the other towering conifers. No, it must be the aspen, a tree discreet in summer and inexistent in winter but which bursts into color in the fall when the dark conifer forests are powdered with specks of pure gold. Some ten thousand years ago, the aspen covered a much wider territory than it does today. With the warming of the atmosphere and the gradual drying-out of the land, it has now retreated into the mountains. The climate has become too dry to guarantee the survival of its tiny

seeds and so it has adopted another strategy, spreading upwards from its roots. All the trees in a given zone come from the same rootstock. The aspen forests form one big family in which each clan can be distinguished from the others by the color of its leaves. During the winter, the deer and porcupines find substantial nourishment in its bark. Because of the chlorophyll pigments it contains, the bark captures light and transforms it into a sap rich in nutritive elements. This process allows the tree to protect its delicate leaves from the whims of an early or late winter. The soft fall light filters through the white boles of an aspen grove. Overhead, the wind breaks into a host of quivers and flutters. Each leaf is a trembling coin of gold or copper, put into currency by the wind. The slopes of the Rockies whisper, the forest makes its voice heard for the last time before the silence of the long winter.

Pale and fragile, the aspens stretch up to clothe the slopes of the Elk Mountains in Colorado. Unremarkable in winter and summer, the aspens burst into color in the fall just before the chill winds strip their branches and scatter their wealth.

Before the poplars have time to shed their autumn colors,
winter tightens its cold grip on the San Juan Mountains in Colorado and on Wyoming's Grand Tetons.

WINTER, LORD OF THE MOUNTAINS

More than any other season, winter leaves the deepest mark on the Rocky mountains. Winter continues to shape all forms of life inside its kingdom of snow. With the first blasts of October wind, winter stakes its claim to the land, pushing out the fall.

grass, all the while protected from most predators by a comforting roof of snow. Some serious dangers may be on the prowl however. Ermines, perfectly camouflaged except for their tail-tip, plunge into the powdery snow in pursuit of these burrowers.

The last flurries of snow often curtail nest-building in June and push back the arrival of spring into July. Up in the mountains the annual snowfall ranges from 30 to 45 feet, blanketing the slopes with a heavy white comforter. For many plants and little animals, this quilt is a real protection, safeguarding their delicate roots or warm blood while, up above, temperatures continue to fall and the winds blow colder. Winter doesn't necessarily mean lethargy or drowsiness for everyone. It can also be a time of vital activity. Chipmunks, those short-eared little balls of fur with an ebullient personality, dig labyrinths to go dine on frozen plants before returning to their chambers stuffed with dried

Up on the surface, coyotes with ears like antennas wait ready to snap up the slightest opportunity. Only the woodchucks and certain species of ground squirrels, professional hibernators, manage to sleep their way through these potential dangers. Although heavily burdened by the weight of the snow, the undergrowth remains active. Bluebirds and nuthatches investigate mossy trunks, probing for insect grubs and eggs. Higher in the branches, finches strip pine cones to reach the kernels. During the long winter months, the aspen bark and the long willow catkins are the only food available to browsers like the moose, mule deer and other deer.

The Yellowstone River has cut a deep canyon through the rhyolite volcanic rock,
leaving pinnacles which erosion continues to sharpen.

Highly mineralized boiling springs bubble in basins ringed with lacy concretions,
even in the depths of winter. Yellowstone National Park, Wyoming.

THE BIG BANG

Yellowstone was born of gigantic volcanic explosions. The most recent - and most violent - rocked the area 600,000 years ago. Over thousands of years, the magma had been accumulating in a gigantic underground reservoir. Subjected to overwhelming pressure, the lava finally burst through the thin crust of the earth in this zone, blowing a thousand cubic kilometres of rock into the air. As the molten rock was thrown out, the roof of the subterranean chamber once containing it caved in, leaving what we call a caldera. This crater, or cauldron, measuring 45 miles long by 30 wide, forms the central part of Yellowstone as we know it today. Vulcanologists have calculated that over the past two million years, the region has thrown out as much lava as, for example, Hawaii or Iceland. When the caldera was created, in the space of, most probably, two or three days, the volume of molten rock blown out could have blanketed a country the size of France with a layer over six feet deep. Although no new seismic activity has taken place since, the earth still rumbles menacingly under Yellowstone. Lava continues to accumulate and the earth's crust is swelling with the pressure. No one can say when the next explosions are likely to occur but, judging from the past, they should be spectacular.

THE UNION OF FIRE AND WATER

It's not easy to decipher the traces of these ancient telluric disruptions in today's landscape. Yet the ponds of turquoise water, the siliceous terraces, the geysers and the sulfur springs remain the principal attractions which bring some three million visitors a year to the park. In Yellowstone, the visitor can explore geological time, discovering uncompleted landscapes and seeing how fire and water combine to fashion the land. This idea of a landscape in motion is fascinating and the visitor suddenly realizes that what he had thought was inert, his earth, is in fact a living creature. He hears deep rumblings come reverberating up from the nether regions, feels the ground tremble around the geysers, smells the sharp whiff of brimstone in the air, wipes the hot vapor sticking to his skin and stares, mesmerized, at the fantastic colors around the pools of turquoise water. All his senses experience new and disquieting sensations. Yellowstone national park is the region with the world's largest concentration of hydrothermal activity. There are practically three hundred geysers and over ten thousand post-volcanic phenomena. This is where the world's most famous geyser puts on a show, before an expectant crowd, every day at regularly spaced intervals. Old Faithful has never let its public down. Twenty-two times daily, it sprays out over 10,000 gallons of hot water and steam vapor at intervals of between 55 and 80 minutes depending on the quantity of water and steam in the underground vents. Old Faithful almost had the limelight stolen from it when, in 1978, a competitor named the Steamboat blew jets of vapor over 350 feet into the air, qualifying it as the world's highest geyser. All through the park, the earth seems determined to reveal its underground mysteries. Sulfurous smoke and gas waft up from solfataras, these basins where the rock is reduced to magma by the heat rising from volcanic chimneys and colored by a whole spectrum of oxidations. A black soup smelling of brimstone bubbles in great cauldrons. The compressed gases in these cauldrons give off bubbles with the heat which rise to burst on the surface with sticky plopping noises. The hot springs feed the rivers which never freeze, even in the depths of winter, and along whose banks the deer and buffalo prefer to graze. At Mammoth Hot Springs, the siliceous and mineral-laden waters leave a fine, whitish crust every day which gradually builds up to form delicately colored, lacework terraces. The rainbow colors around the banks of Grand Prismatic Spring are

left by microscopic living organisms which, unbelievably, manage to thrive in the scalding waters. Known as thermophiles, they are perfectly adapted to life in conditions which would kill all other forms. The color spectrum comes from an elaborate combination of various bacteria, algae, minerals and their own luminous reflection. Yellowstone national park lives in constant mutation and its ecosystems have to adapt accordingly.

Pumped up from the depths of the earth,
Yellowstone's Mammoth Hot Springs are laden with minerals such as geyserite
which they deposit in a cascade of shimmering basins.

Phantom landscape of a pine forest ravaged by the natural-ignition fires which swept through Yellowstone in the summer of 1988 on a scale never seen before.

THE YELLOWSTONE FIRES

Following a particularly mild winter and an almost-total absence of rainfall, the summer of 1988 saw natural-ignition fires sweep through Yellowstone on an unprecedented scale in the history of the park service. Some bolts of summer lightning, a few sparks and the fire began to burn. Fanned by strong winds, the flames were soon advancing at a speed of 14 miles a day, jumping the roads and vaulting across the Grand Canyon of the Yellowstone river. Eight huge infernos ravaged 1.4 million acres in and around the park. Because of their intensity, their length and the difficulties they caused firefighters, these Yellowstone fires were later described as the most exceptional event to have happened in the history of the American national parks. Yet were they an ecological disaster? Should the fire have been fought or was it better to have let it burn itself out? The truth is that these fires were 'a fabulous stimulant' and, according to one of the park's administrators, 'as important for an ecosystem as the sun and the rain'.

Over a decade later, it is hard to believe, standing in the midst of charred trees, that life has continued. Yet if we look closer, we begin to see the regenerative power of fires like these. The burned trunks have fertilized the soil, space has been opened for young growth, light is allowed in to help these shoots and the number of plant species has increased, thereby triggering an upsurge in the food chain. Up until 1972, park policy was to sys-

tematically extinguish all fires. Scientists began to notice that natural fires played an essential ecological role in regulating ecosystems. The lodgepole pines which make up some 80% of Yellowstone's forest produce two types of cones, some which open at maturity, scattering their seeds, and others, known as serotinous, which open only when exposed to intense heat. Thus the fire allows millions of seeds to escape and recolonize the soil. Five years after the great fires, the ground was already covered with pine seedlings. In fact, the 1988 fires underlined the supreme power of Mother Nature. For some, this policy of non-intervention is slowly killing the park, but according to its biologists, Yellowstone's life cycle has never been so healthy and vigorous. The debate is an old one, dating back to the old days when the wolf returned to Yellowstone and his howling once more sent shivers down the spines of campers cosily installed in their bivouacs

Buffalo and elk come to graze where the heat from the springs and the solfataras has melted the winter snows. Yellowstone National Park.

These ocher-yellow walls of the Yellowstone canyon,
pictured here just down from the Lower Falls, gave the park its name.

4

THE WEST

Deserts and Indian Lands

"No human imagination,
even nourished with all manner of descriptions,
can depict the beauty and wild character of the scenes which unfold
daily before my eyes in these romantic lands."

George Catlin,
American artist (1796-1872)

◁ *Like a window onto another world for the Indians, this sandstone arch frames the*
unique landscape of Monument Valley Navajo Tribal Park. Arizona/Utah.

The sand dunes of Mesquite Flat shift with the strong winds which sweep through this driest region of the United States.
Death Valley National Park, California.

The West had impregnated the American imagination even before these landscapes were known. Applying his theory of the frontier, the American historian F.J. Turner presented the West as a region of unoccupied, virgin soil, ripe for the advancement of colonization and the development of America. The Land of Eagles, as its first inhabitants baptized it, was a dry land, but rich in Indian communities. Hundreds in all, they had learned to adapt to this pitiless environment, to extract their living from its slightest encouragements. Unencumbered by any notion of property, the main preoccupation of these Indians was to 'take care of the land and the sky'. A land of exile for many, the West soon became, when gold was discovered, a land of asylum. Many decades later, the movie industry used these mesas of red sandstone, these pinnacles and buttes sculpted by wind and water, these bottomless canyons of Colorado, Utah, Arizona and New Mexico as backdrops, thereby perpetuating the legend of the Far West

Among the many Anasazi sites in the Four Corners region, New Mexico's Chaco Canyon became the most flourishing religious and cultural center of a civilization which suddenly disappeared. Chetro Ketl, New Mexico & Canyon de Chelly National Monument, Arizona.

*Mineral oxidizations of cobalt,
manganese and iron form the different hues of Artist's Palette in the badlands
of Death Valley, New Mexico/California.*

THE WESTERN DESERTS: A QUESTION OF DEFINITION

Deserts which aren't really deserts, objected Théodore Monod, who preferred the term 'semi-arid regions' to define these high and low lands, secondary ranges and basins, salt-whitened playas with their cracked, parched earth, their shining mesas, their cactus gardens and their dusty flats swept by the tumbleweed. According to the pre-eminent French specialist, only California's famous Death Valley and the delta of the Colorado, down in Mexico, qualify as true deserts with the necessary degree of dryness. In these normally temperate latitudes, the curious desert phenomenon is caused by the high summits of the Sierra Nevada barring the way for the Pacific rainclouds. Without consensus on the exact limits of these semi-arid regions, biologists have divided the 300,000 square miles of 'North American deserts' into several units. The Great Basin, the highest and the most northerly, is the coolest of all. The Chihuahua Desert, North America's largest, spreads from Mexico into the extreme western reaches of Texas and the south of New Mexico, encompassing the White Sands National Monument and Big Bend National Park. This essentially scrub desert is characterized by low winter temperatures and baking hot summers. The drier Mojave Desert receives less than an inch and a half of rain on average every year. It covers the southern part of Nevada, the south-western corner of Utah and part of California. The out-stretched arms of the arborescent yucca, which reminded the Mormons of the prophet Joshua, are a familiar feature of the Joshua Tree National

These sand dunes were deposited, thousands of years ago,
by the south-eastern winds blowing over the passes of the Sangre de Cristo mountains.
Great Sand Dunes National Monument, Colorado.

Adapting to many climatic changes down through the centuries,
the oldest bristlecone pines live for up to 6000 years. Long after their death, the wood remains astonishingly resistant.
Great Basin National Park, Nevada.

Prickly pears, mesquite and creosote bushes thrive on the thin soils ▷
and dry climate of Arizona's Sonoran Desert

Monument in California. These curious trees are the most emblematic representatives of a desert famous for the diversity of its plant life.

Down, down, ever downwards into a furnace, the slopes of the Panamint Mountains seem endless, taking us down towards this blue-tinged mirage which raises hopes of some inland sea whereas the temperature keeps increasing. In full summer, the floor of Death Valley evaporates in the heat, rising to meet us. Even the silence is burning. The bitter, sulfur-tainted odor of this huge brackish lake, dry for most of the year, burns in the visitor's nostrils. At 280 feet below sea level, in the heart of this playa, Badwater ranks as the lowest point in North America. With an annual rainfall of around one and a half inches and a ground temperature 40% higher than the surrounding atmosphere, Death Valley meets all the conditions for hyper-aridity. The most extensive desert in the United States, the Sonora covers south-western Arizona, south-eastern California and the western half of the Mexican state of Sonora. Despite its furnace temperatures, it is blessed with winter and summer rains and hosts a very wide variety of plant life. With over six hundred species, including two hundred and fifty different wildflowers and over a hundred varieties of cacti, this desert is a garden whose colors change with the seasons. Spring bursts out in late March in Saguaro and Organ Pipe Cactus, Arizona's national monuments, and California's Anza Borego. The atmosphere quickens with the humming of the insects, the song of the birds and the heady scent of the desert flowers. In this arid environment, spring is so transient that plants and animals have developed remarkable survival techniques. The desert plants face the dual problem of how to attract pollinators and how to

defend themselves against hungry rodents and other mammals. Among these xeric plants, adapted to drought conditions, the cacti have solved these difficulties by producing brilliantly colored blooms protected by a hedge of spines, bristles or hooks. Gila woodpeckers, mourning doves, cactus wrens and mockingbirds take turns to come harvest the abundant pollen and the many insects attracted by the flowers, anxious to feed their chicks before the choking summer heat evaporates food supplies and shade. Nests are built directly on the cactus spines or in cavities dug into the trunk of the saguaros, hidden from the eyes of predators and sheltered from the direct rays of the sun. Although principally occupied by the question of feeding their broods, the birds keep a wary eye out for predators. Coyotes, bobcats, little desert foxes and the occasional mountain lion take advantage of the relative spring coolness and the abundant prey to hunt in broad daylight. Cholla, prickly pear and other cactuses plumed with golden flowers rub spiny shoulders with white or green fuchsias amid carpets of thick grass and clumps of verbena, desert anemones, marigolds and little golden zinnias. Mexican poppies, blue lupins and scrophularia form colorful masses on the higher ground and the rocky slopes. This season of growth and plenty passes all too quickly; the thermometer rises, evaporation increases and the nights are no longer cool. Even the jackrabbit slows down and all living creatures bend to the inexorably slow rhythm of desert life. Predators resume their nocturnal habits. Bushes, cactuses and ocotillos dry out rapidly. The ground begins to fissure and the desert slips off its spring mask to reveal its true face, the face its inhabitants will see until the rains begin again.

The hedgehog cactus vies with the brittlebrush
when spring visits the Superstition Mountains of the Sonoran Desert.

Cluster of palms in the Anza Borrego desert.

Clusters of heavy greenish-white flowers crown these Joshua Trees against a backdrop
of granite boulders in California's Joshua Tree National Monument.

The petroglyphs on Signal Hill portray animals which once roamed the Sonoran region.
Saguaro National Monument, Arizona.

Sap still runs up the tortured, iron-hard trunks
of these ancient bristlecone pines growing in the desert wastelands of the Sierra Nevada.
Great Basin National Park, Nevada.

At the close of winter,
torrential rains continue to flood the badlands in California's Anza Borrego Desert State Park.

THE SAGUARO: LIFE AND DEATH OF A SONORAN MONARCH

The saguaro seedling begins life as a tiny black seed. Just one, out of the thousands which the saguaro produces every year. Just one shiny little seed develops, growing in the shade of a paloverde or a mesquite, where it finds the necessary protection and humidity. This foster parent screens it from the birds and the rodents, helping it survive its long childhood. A saguaro grows infinitely slowly. At fifteen years old, it is barely a foot tall and its first branches grow at the age of seventy-five. During these long years, the saguaro ungratefully soaks up the water reserves of its foster parent until the latter's death from thirst. The first flowers blossom at the same time as the first branches. Tight corollas, swollen with pollen, sprout from the tips of the

branches and open at night. Their fragrance is so powerful that it carries for miles in the night air, attracting famished bats who, as they lap up the pollen, also act as pollinators for their hosts. With its accordion folds, the saguaro swells to store the water gathered by its long, shallow roots, transforming it into a whitish gelatine. While protecting the plant from animals tempted to tap these reserves, the cactus spines also slow the process of evaporation. Like an idol with feet of clay, this fragile giant, who can stretch to up to sixty feet high and weigh over eight tons, is easily unsettled by violent winds. The arborescent cactus is also a victim of human encroachment, seeing its forests whittled away by pastureland and its habitat criss-crossed by roads. When the Sonoran monarch dies still upright, its skeleton remains standing, the remains of its pulpy flesh preserved in the dry desert air.

A delicate balance of winter rainfall, warmth, wind and soil humidity
enables the desert plants to flower each spring. The saguaro cactus blooms come out at night
and fade as the day goes on. Lupins and brittlebrush surround an organ-pipe cactus
in Arizona's national monument of the same name.

When siting their kiva,
did the Anasazi need any other reason than this sweeping view over the Green River canyon?
Canyonlands National Park, Utah.

Descendants of the horses brought across by the Spanish conquistadors,
the mustangs have adapted to the arid environment of the American west.
Monument Valley, Utah/Arizona.

The snowflakes drifting past this south rim of the Grand Canyon have another mile to go,
down to the river below. Arizona.

Solidly anchored into fissures in the rock, snow-covered junipers look out over the meanders of the Green River.
Canyonlands National Park, Utah.

MESAS, ARCHES AND CANYONS: DECORS FOR WESTERNS ON LOCATION

Sandstone plateaux smooth as tabletops, vertical lines of sheer cliffs, gentle slopes of erosion aprons and the round, voluptuous forms of water-worn rock... chaotic piles of boulders, pedestals, red-rock reliefs, sandstone towers bristling in wide valleys... the weathered landscapes of the West are the stone memories of a tumultuous geological past. When the sea at last withdrew from the region, after so many advances and retreats, leaving a bed of sediment dozens of yards deep, the forces of erosion set to work on this petrified ocean, probing the weaknesses of the rock, filtering into its pores, capturing its weak heart and splitting apart its tiniest fissures. This mortal combat between insiduous water and last-stand rock is written large on the horizon of the far west. An immemorial river, born in the Rockies, has cut through the Colorado plateau, building temples, minarets, spires of sandstone and levelling others. The Colorado has gouged deep canyons and wide oxbows, endowing the region with geological curiosities which are now the attractions of some of the land's most famous national parks. In a rolling wave of petrified dunes, Arches National Park protects over five hundred natural bridges carved in the Utah sandstone. Open windows onto another world for the Navajo Indians, these arches are the result of tectonic movements which split thick layers of sandstone laid on a bed of salt. Water and frost widened these fissures so much that the walls of sandstone grew thinner and thinner until they finally opened. Over the centuries, these openings grew into the soaring arches which gave the park its name. Not without difficulty, the Green river finally joined the Colorado in what is now the Canyonlands Park, cutting its way in a series of wandering curves to leave what the Spanish called tables, *the mesas,* flat-topped islands of stone floating in the changing light of the sky. Towards the mountains, the red rock of Utah reserves other surprises: Bryce Canyon, an immense amphitheater where crumbly rock powdered with ocher and red-brown rust continues to cede ground to water and wind erosion, and Zion, where the overwhelming presence of the flaming cliffs and the fall colors of the poplar groves leave the canyon mouths dark and mysterious. Farther south, the Colorado cuts a channel a mile deep, as if searching for the origins of the earth, to form the Grand Canyon, the most visited of the American national parks. The West is a cliché abused by filmmakers and expected by audiences. Yet, historically, the desert wastes of Utah, Arizona, Nevada and a part of California were never the scenes of territorial struggles. These regions were mainly the refuges of Indians, outlaws and Mormons, marginal populations who did not fit into the hardening mold of American civilization. The movie industry created a historical transformation, a sort of visual falsification of the true sites of the history of the West, by substituting the conventional desert landscapes in their films. The true territorial battles were elsewhere, farther north along the trails of Wyoming, much farther south and more to the east, along the tracks of the railroad. John Ford was the first to use the desert as a backdrop, filming in Monument Valley with a wide-angle lens to create the notion of wide open spaces and underscore the idea of movement. The western is escapist cinema, a change of scenery and a distant echo of the real conquest of the West.

Backdrop scenery to so many westerns, the landscapes of Monument Valley evoke all the conflicts linked to the conquest of the west. Navajo Tribal Park, Utah/Arizona.

As worn and eroded as the pinnacles of Bryce Canyon,
the trunk of this bristlecone pine owes its mimetic color to the lichens which colonize it.
Bryce Canyon National Park, Utah.

Now controlled by a huge hydroelectric complex,
the waters of the Colorado flow peacefully between the towering walls it has carved.
Grand Canyon National Park, Arizona.

A bighorn sheep looks down from the safety of the park's boulder-strewn hillsides.

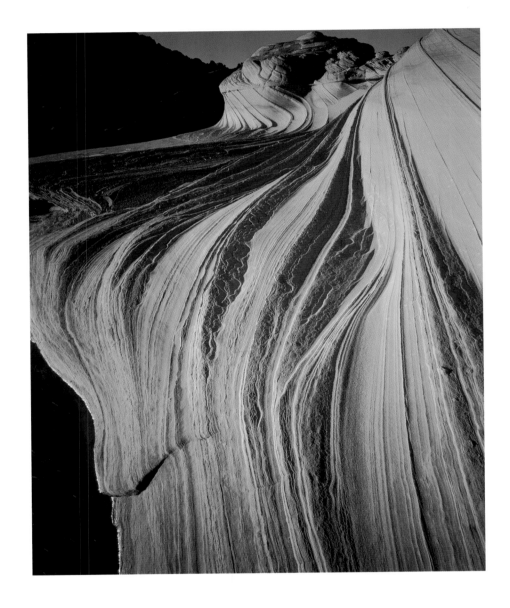

The flowing drapery of the Navajo sandstone lit by the slanting rays of the setting sun.
Vermilion Cliffs Wilderness, Arizona.

Delicate Arch, daughter of the land and the wind, spans the snow-capped peaks of the La Sal mountains.
Arches National Park, Utah.

THE ROADRUNNER, FASTEST LEGS IN THE WEST

A flash of lightning streaks across the red trail. A rustle in the bushes and the dust begins to dissipate in the overheated air, revealing faint tracks in the dirt, already beginning to smudge. *Geococcyx californianus,* the roadrunner, just crossed in front of the pickup. A lucky sign, according to the Mexicans. He stops a little way into the scrub, waiting under a mesquite bush. Like all serious running birds, this member of the cuckoo family is equipped with long legs ending in relatively short toes. His disproportionately long tail serves as a rudder, allowing him to zig-zag at full speed. His wings are stubby but, given his preference for running, it doesn't really matter; he flaps away, low over the bushes, only in cases of red alert. Tail extended horizontally, long beak pointing full ahead and crest laid back, he's off again, his legs a mere blur. His specialities? Long-distance running and sprints, where he has been

timed at 20 miles an hour. He is also an accomplished long-jumper, able to clear nine feet when hunting. This avian athlete lives in the arid regions of the south-western United States and Mexico. With his clown allure and his cartoon fame, the legendary roadrunner is immediately recognizable and everybody has heard of him. Yet his speckled plumage, a tweedy mix of beige, white and metallic green, is an excellent camouflage, hiding him most effectively in the dappled light and shade of mesquite and creosote scrub. While crickets and large quantities of snails constitute the staples of his diet, the roadrunner is also a master of the art of hunting lizards and snakes, quartering his territory to flush them out and even daring attack young rattlesnakes. To avoid their venom, he attacks the snake's head, feignting with his wings. Once vanquished by his opponent's rapier beak, the snake is swallowed, head first, and the victor often resumes his normal activities with a portion of the snake's body hanging from his beak, ready to be consumed later when his crop is ready for a second helping. How does a bird who should limit his efforts to survive in a desert environment find so much energy? As soon as the huge orange ball of the sun rises above the pale horizon, the roadrunner comes out of the hypothermia he sinks into at night to protect himself from the cold and immediately searches for a clear, open space in the scrub. Here he turns his back to the sun, spreads his wings and lifts the feathers of his back to let the sun act on the dark skin underneath, storing the heat like a solar panel. One hour of sunning later, our Californian runner is recharged again and ready to be off.

*The roadrunner takes a sunbath every morning to warm him out
of his nocturnal hypothermia.*

*Fastest bird in the west,
this roadrunner is hurrying home to his nest with the lizard just caught.*

*Many trails from other communities converge towards Pueblo Bonito,
an Anasazi city built on a semi-circular plan for probably religious purposes.* ▷
Chaco Culture National Historical Park, New Mexico.

*Anasazi petroglyphs on the sandstone walls of Chaco Canyon.
Chaco Culture National Historical Park, New Mexico.*

LAND OF THE ANCIENTS

Three great Indian cultures dominated the pre-historic south-west. The Hohokam (literally 'those who have gone'), who lived in the valleys which cut across the Sonoran desert around the present city of Phoenix, were an agricultural society. They were the first in this region to set up a system of irrigation, digging channels alongside the Gila and Salt rivers to water their crops of corn, beans, cotton and agave. Casa Grande, a four-storey adobe tower and the most celebrated vestige of their civilization, is reputed to have been an astronomical observatory. The Mogollon derived their name from the New Mexican mountains. These hunter-gatherers wandered across a vast territory spreading over

Texas, New Mexico and Arizona. When no game was available, they lived on a diet of nuts, seeds, fruit and cactus. Particularly inventive, they were the first in the south-west to make pottery. The Gila Cliff Dwellings national monument in New Mexico preserves the remains of their third and last period of occupation. Did these people die out? Did they drift away northwards? Or was the Mogollon civilization absorbed by the Anasazi, those superb cliff architects? The name Anasazi means 'ancient enemies' (or perhaps simply 'ancients') in the Navajo language, but we have no idea what they called themselves. The Spanish conquerors called them 'the village people' or Pueblos, because they

built houses. Whatever their name, the soul of the Anasazi can still be captured in the Four Corners country, in the national monuments of Arizona's Canyon de Chelly and Navajo, Utah/Colorado's Hovenweep and the fabulous cities of Chaco Canyon and Mesa Verde.

Archaeologists now confirm that this elegant building construction technique,
used for half the walls of Pueblo Bonito, was covered with rendering.
Chaco Culture National Historical Park.

In Hovenweep National Monument, between Utah and Colorado,
the Anasazi dwellings were built in the depths of the canyons, near springs of drinking water.
The surrounding cliffs had no natural caves that could be used as refuges.

MESA VERDE

THE CITY OF THE ANASAZI

Heavy flakes of snow piled up on the frozen ground. Blanketed in white, the forests of piñon pines and junipers blended into the pale winter sky, completing a perfect frame for the ocher cliffs. Two cowboys, Benjamin Alfred Wetherill and his brother-in-law Charlie Mason, were driving some cattle they'd lost the day before, looking at the canyon walls as they rode. For some time now, they'd been looking for proof of an improbable story the Ute Indians, their neighbors back at the ranch, had told them. A story of very

ancient Indian ruins built into the cliffs. But suppose it were true, suppose they did find those famous cities in the towering cliffs of this region? On this December 18th 1888, their curiosity was rewarded when Ben, squinting into the bitter wind, suddenly distinguished the ruins of a 'magnificent city' on the cliff opposite. These ranchers from the Mancos region were the first white men to discover the ruins of the Cliff Palace, as they baptized it. After exploring the surrounding area, they entered the dwellings and gathered a small collection of objects. On their way back, they also found the Spruce Tree house and the Square Tower house. This discovery soon changed their lives; Alamo ranch became a tourist destination and the two men redeployed themselves as tour guides for an ever-increasing stream of visitors. A journalist named Virginia Donaghe McClurg began a campaign to call public attention to the need to protect these rock-dwellings from incessant pillage. Her call was heard by other female militants. The ladies banded together, began negotiations with the Ute Indians and finally convinced Congress to create the Mesa Verde National Park in June 1906, the first cultural site to be thus protected.

Some 1500 years ago, the Anasazi Indians set up home in the natural rock shelters of Mesa Verde.
Seven centuries later, this seemingly flourishing civilization mysteriously disappeared from the region.
Cliff Palace Mesa, Colorado.

With its 217 rooms and 23 ceremonial kivas,
Mesa Verde's Cliff Palace was the largest Anasazi construction built against the cliff.
Mesa Verde National Park, Colorado.

The coati, a near cousin to the raccoon, probes the vegetation with his long,
flexible snout in search of fruit, seeds, scorpions or the occasional lizard.

*The ruins of the White House tell of a peaceful era
which encouraged the Anasazi to choose this site. Upon the arrival of the Europeans,
the Navajo sought refuge in the Canyon de Chelly where they still live to this day.
Canyon de Chelly National Monument, Arizona.*

Autumn colors burn a trail to the White House ruins beneath their beetling sandstone cliffs. ▷
Canyon de Chelly National Monument, Arizona.

THE GREEN TABLELAND

Accounts of the early Spanish expeditions already mention 'the green table'. This great plateau, 6000 to 7000 feet high, rises to the west of the Rockies, in present-day Colorado. It is made up of a thick layer of sandstone, scarred with canyons running parallel north-south to join the Mancos river. The semi-arid climate, coupled with the altitude, produces a mountain-type vegetation of scrub bushes with drought-resistant species hanging from the cliffs. The Douglas firs occupy the high ground, leaving the lower slopes to the mountain

mahogany, ash and Gambel oaks. Junipers and piñon pines cover the mesas and the canyon slopes. The vegetation in the generally dry valleys is denser, composed of sage-brush, tomatillos and prickly pears. The rare Peale's falcon has reappeared and now nests again on the cliffs, frightening the cawing crows. The black bear, the lynx and the mountain goat are, on the other hand, much rarer sights. This diversity of plant and wildlife, together with the defensive possibilities of this sheltered environment, attracted the Anasazi farmer-gatherers.

THE ANASAZI, ARCHITECTS OF MESA VERDE

They lacked neither space nor soil suitable for cultivation. They even had naturally-protected sites with commanding views to use as refuges. So why did the Anasazi choose to cling to abrupt, even sheer cliffs in the middle of this arid environment? Was it fear or attraction? The question remains a mystery which archaeologists still seek to unravel. Between 1100 and 1300 AD, the classic Mesa Verde period, the 'Old Ones' abandoned their carefully laid-out villages on the sunny mesas to move into open-mouthed caves midway up the dizzy canyon walls. Experts have distinguished several periods in this civilization, from Basketmaker I through III and then from Pueblo I through V. Already, around the year 700 AD, the lifestyle of this people had undergone a major transformation. The pit-houses they had dug as dwellings were gradually replaced by masonry buildings above ground. Their agricultural yields increased, encouraged by more sophisticated techniques. This was the period when the kivas began to appear, circular underground chambers used for worship and community meetings. Over the years between 1100 and 1250, the population expanded. In rock shelters and on the mesa tops, they carried stones and heavy logs up ladders to build temples and square towers - daring constructions of

four, even five storeys, containing dozens of rooms - on narrow terraces. Unlike the elegant edifices of Chaco Canyon, another magnificent Anasazi citadel in New Mexico, the villages of Mesa Verde seem to follow no clear plan. The cliff houses are built vertically as independent structures and then successively interconnected by terraces. The city of Far View, on Chaplin Mesa, was founded around 900. Two hundred years later it had grown to engulf eighteen other villages and boasted a population of 500 inhabitants. In the Mesa Verde National Park, Cliff Palace, one of North America's greatest cave-dwellers' settlements, contained 217 rooms and 23 kivas for an estimated population of 250. Some six hundred cave dwellings have been protected within this park, some built 500 feet above the canyon floor. Population growth during this period prompted the Anasazi to venture farther afield and settle on the highlands of the Colorado plateau, building villages like Keet Seel or the Canyon de Chelly's White House in Arizona.

After barely fifty years in these new cliff dwellings, the Anasazi suddenly vanished from the entire south-west when some new crisis struck. Since the discovery of these sites over a century ago, many hypotheses have been put forward to explain this sudden exodus, most involving climatic changes. Recent discoveries by a generation of young archaeologists have opened up new lines of thought. Particularly extended and repeated periods of drought probably played a role in the population shift from the arid Chaco region to the cooler cliffs of Mesa Verde, later abandoned in their turn. Many skeletons attest to the

harsh living conditions of the time. Yet for too long archaeologists considered the desertion of these sites as a flight, never stopping to consider that it could have been a free-will decision, dictated by some irresistible attraction elsewhere. Some fascinating religion, for example, may have prompted the Indians to leave their cliffs and the Colorado uplands and migrate hundreds of miles southwards and east, abandoning their ceremonial rooms, their grandiose citadels and leaving us with the tantalizing clues of pottery, jewelry, seeds and baskets to try to piece together this mysterious civilization.

Tucked away under a gigantic sandstone arch,
the Anasazi ruins of Keet Seel, in Arizona's Navajo National Monument, are marvelously well preserved.

The looming cliffs of Paria Canyon color the waters which carved them.
Vermilion Cliffs Wilderness, Arizona.

◁ *The mysterious Fremont Indians cut these petroglyphs into the colored walls of*
Capitol Reef National Park in Utah.

5

THE PACIFIC COAST

A misty shoreline

*"To become a sequoia,
out there with only the mountains and the empty sky,
let the centuries flow over you like some delicate wave,
store the memory of the earth in your roots and
catch the clouds in your branches"*

*Michel Lebris,
contemporary French author*

◁ *Forest-covered islets torn from the coast by the power of the ocean.
Olympic National Park, Washington.*

The sandy beaches of Point Reyes give way to an impressive line of windswept cliffs
where only the hardiest vegetation manages to survive.
Point Reyes National Seashore, California.

Early November 1805. A distant booming, like far-off music, suddenly reached the ears of the pioneers on the Lewis and Clark expedition. The long-awaited Pacific surged inland in great rollers, tossing huge tree trunks in the estuary of the Columbia river. The expedition battled their way downriver against the estuary for eleven days, finally arriving at the ocean on November 15th.

"Ocean in sight, oh what joy!" wrote Clark in his notebook on reaching the Pacific. Yet despite this joy, the north-west coast of America gave them a cold welcome: freezing winds, difficult camping conditions and "nothing to eat except pounded fish". The ocean is pacific only in name. It rages against the western shoreline of North America, shrouds it permanently in dense fog and lashes it with rain. In self-defence, the coast has developed a rugged, untamed character. Temperate forests and, notably, coast redwoods, thrive in this waterlogged atmosphere. In the Hawaiian archipelago and in the Cascade Range, still quivering from the shock of Mount Saint Helens, the earth remains unsteady, temperamental and incandescent. Winter lays a heavy hand on the Sierra Nevada, those magnificent mountains which have inspired so many artists.

The upsurges of warmer water stirred by the Pacific
bring a welcome breakfast for the gulls along Drake's Beach.
Point Reyes National Seashore, California.

*Fringed with beargrass, Reflection Lake lives up to its name
and mirrors the snowy summit of Mount Rainier, second highest peak in the lower 48 states.
Mount Rainier National Park, Washington.*

THE SIERRA NEVADA, MOUNTAINS OF LIGHT

Overshadowed by Mount Whitney, the highest peak in the contiguous United States, the Sierra Nevada boasts the southernmost glaciers in North America. The world's largest tree, the towering sequoia, grows on its slopes. Yet despite its majestic peaks, its sparkling snows, its awesome ravines, its dark forests and its deep lakes, the soul of the Sierra is more subtle than spectacular. In this region, where the uplands are shared between the sky, the snow and the bare rock, the sunlight meets no impediment. The atmosphere is clear and light. The pure light washed by the storms of the Pacific or the soft light reflected from the polished rock?

What gives these Sierra landscapes their special glow? Is it perhaps simply that our eyes are opened wider by their sheer magnificence? The Sierra of the 19th century, so dear to John Muir, is the same as today's Sierra: mountains of light. It extends the Cascade Range southwards, a long wall almost 350 miles long. The western face traps all the humidity carried on the winds from the Pacific. Clad with thick forests, it is totally different from the eastern face, which, particularly sheer, overlooks the desert and contents itself with the rains the peaks have allowed over. On the sedimentary slopes of the White Mountains grows one of the world's oldest

*California boasts the lowest (Death Valley) and the highest points
in the contiguous United States. At 14,491 feet, Mount Whitney towers over the Sierra Nevada
in the early rays of the morning sun.*

trees, the bristlecone pine, *Pinus longaeva,* an antediluvian survivor whose silky cones embalm warm days with the scent of resin, the fresh, sweet tang of youth. They seem unaffected by the passing centuries and their lifeforce is exemplary: the harder the conditions - poor soil, drought, cold, ice - the more resistant they become. Even when the trunk seems dead, the life force continues in a tiny sliver of bark. And when finally it flutters out, the elegant skeletons still stand for thousands of years; the wood erodes slowly, polished by the wind and the cold. This ancient survivor, a venerable 4700 years old, looks down on most giant sequoias[4] as mere saplings.

Ghostly silhouettes of a grove of ancient Monterey cypresses in the Pacific mist along Point Reyes National Seashore, California.

'Eternal God, a redwood in California's Prairie Creek Redwoods State Park, is reputed to be an incredible 12,000 years old.

Even older, these bristlecone pines welcome yet another dawn
over the White Mountains of California.

THE SEQUOIA, A VEGETAL COLOSSUS

Towering, outsize, gigantic, colossal... no adjective is strong enough to describe the giant sequoia, the most monumental of all the living species known on earth. Its ancestors once shaded the lumbering dinosaurs. The present-day giant sequoias have found a last refuge here, in the central Sierra, where they grow in a narrow strip at an altitude of between 4000 and 7000 feet where the rainfall is abundant and the winters not too harsh. Overlooking all the other species on these slopes, they

are the last to feel the moist fingers of the rising mists and the first to whiten with the snowflakes in winter. The discovery of these vegetal giants made news around the world in 1852 and the timber contractors immediately began calculating the staggering number of outsize planks each trunk could furnish. Too stringy for fine joinery or cabinetmaking, the sequoia wood was used to produce fence posts and pencils for Europe... paltry endings for such a noble tree. In less than a century, the white man would have razed the forest completely if a small band of staunch defenders had not taken a stand to save it. Once alerted, increasingly outraged public opinion applied pressure to save the Mariposa forest, now lying within the Yosemite national park. In 1890, America's second national park was opened and named Sequoia, 400,000 acres set aside to guarantee the protection of *Sequoiadendron giganteum*.

Faithful companions to the giant redwoods, rhododendrons thrive in the misty depths of these towering forests. Redwood National Park, California.

adverse effect on their overall numbers. But in the early 19th century, the whalers and seal hunters exterminated this helpless marine mammal, melting down its blubber to provide oil for the gold diggers. When hunting finally ceased, the populations were rebuilt up from a small reserve protected in time by the Mexican government on the island of Guadalupe and soon gained ground again in California. This swift recovery after such a wholesale massacre can be explained by the fortunate fact that elephant seals feed at depths rarely frequented by other species. Scientists and naturalists have observed this comeback with immense satisfaction, noting how the elephant seals reclaim possession of the former haunts in ever greater numbers every year.

Male elephant seal defending his territory and his harem.

YOSEMITE

A WORLD-SIZE CATHEDRAL

"The upper basin of the Merced lay spread out before me almost entirely, with its sublime canyons and domes, the dark forests marching up its slopes and its superb range of white peaks pushing deep into the sky. Each of these elements glowed with an aureole of splendor, radiating a beauty which thrilled our flesh to the very bone, like the warm rays of a fire. Never in my life had I contemplated ... such an unlimited treasure-trove of the supreme beauties of the mountains.". On July 15th 1868, John Muir cried aloud and waved his arms *"in a sudden overflow of ecstasy"* on entering the valley of Yosemite.

THE FIRST NATURAL PARK

In 1855, Yosemite was still a trapper region. Roads were unknown and transport was by mule, along sheer, winding trails. It was at this date that the editor (and early tour operator) James M. Hutchings decided to extol the charms of the valley in his *California Magazine.* Tourists began to hike out to the great granite amphitheater - and were welcomed in the rustic hotel, bought by Hutchings, opposite Yosemite Falls. The valley's reputation grew so swiftly that it soon became the principal attraction of the first tourist circuits. John Muir remained under the spell of his first encounter with the site, spending four subsequent years noting, sketching, studying and charting all the wealth and geological curiosities of the region. He was the first to discover the 'living' glaciers and thus prove the glacial origins of the valley. *'A shepherd's idea'* had replied Josiah D. Whitney, one of the official geologists of the day, in a fit of pique when Muir cast doubt on his cataclysmic explanation for this great gorge. In 1864, Congress and President Abraham Lincoln accepted to protect the Yosemite valley and the Mariposa Grove of Big Trees, setting the land aside for *'public use and the leisure of all'* and stipulating that it was to be *'inalienable from this day onwards'.* Thus this region was the first in the country to be specially preserved for future generations. As such, it was to mark a real departure point for the national park system, even though Yosemite was only officially granted the status of National Park in 1890, some eighteen years after Yellowstone. The name of John Muir remains attached to it.

ICE THE LANDSCAPER

There was a time when the region was simply a series of rolling hills, carpeted with forests and criss-crossed by rivers. When the Sierra Nevada was pushed up, the blocks of granite were split open and pushed aside into a new landscape which accelerated the flow of the Merced. The now fast-moving waters of the river began to dig out a deep, narrow canyon. The climate grew colder, around a million years ago, the forests thinned out and a thick blanket of ice covered the region. When the planet finally warmed again, some ten thousand years ago, this ice mantle gradually began to withdraw. The landscapes of Yosemite as we see them today are the result of the combined action of these glaciers and erosion. The flakey granite summits were stripped bare, peeled like onions along the fissures in concentric rings to expose the rounded reliefs we know today as Half Dome, Sentinel

*The Bridalveil Falls seem to float down from the granite cliffs of Yosemite
(pronounced Yos-emitay), the valley of marvels carved by the iron hand of the distant glaciers.
Yosemite National Park, California.*

Dome, South Dome and the others. When an enormous tongue of ice finally melted, the path of the Merced River had formed an oxbow, that U-shaped bend so characteristic of glacial valleys. It now ran slowly and peacefully along a flat bed bordered by towering rock walls. The mythical spur of El Capitan rises vertical to 3600 feet above the valley

floor. Around Tenaya Lake, the rocks are furrowed by the scraping of the blocks torn free and dragged away by the glaciers. Following the grooves, we can chart the direction taken by the retreating glaciers during the great thaw.

THE VALLEY OF EXALTATION

Curving domes, towering sentinels, a wilderness of pinnacles and spires, walls honed to a cutting edge by the wind, sparkling, striated rocks, lunar fields of scree, pebbles worn smooth by the endless flow of peaceful rivers... the soul of Yosemite is translated in stone. Water springs plentiful from the earth and the valley becomes a garden where Creation is re-enacted. Torrents shimmering with light, moss bedewed by diaphanous scarfs of rising mist, the long golden ribbon of the Merced winding through flaxen grasses, water is omnipresent in this landscape. From Glacier Point, the morning view over the frost-powdered valley is breathtaking. At sunset, when a snowstorm whirls against Half Dome,

The Merced River snakes in the perfect oxbows typical of glacial valleys.
Yosemite National Park, California.

Water in motion, as Yosemite Falls tumble down the sheer face of Half Dome,
◁ *and water at rest in the glacial Tenaya Lake with granite erratic boulders on the rocky slopes above it.*
Yosemite National Park, California.

that granite monolith half torn away by a glacier, we stand bewitched. A single ray of sunlight transforms the misty spray of Horsetail Falls into a rain of gold and calls us back. Back, again and again, because the wonder never palls. Other than a band of early trappers, the first white man to discover the valley, a scout detached from a troop chasing Indian rebels in 1851, underwent a violent shock, *"I felt my whole being filled with a strange exaltation, and my eyes, with emotion, brimmed with tears.".* Painters, philosophers, nature-lovers, backpackers, climbers, fishermen and photographers have since

followed in the footsteps of this chance discoverer, all irresistibly attracted by the beauty of the site. One of them, one who *"spent his time photographing stones while the world was going to pieces",* as Henri Cartier-Bresson said of him, was Ansel Adams, a marvelous interpreter of nature in black and white. At the age of twelve, having spent a vacation in Yosemite valley, Adams left his heart there. Several years later, he gave up a promising career as a professional pianist to devote his life to photography, gradually becoming one of the legendary figures of the valley - and photographer laureate. In his stark monochrome vision, Adams sought to catch that elusive instant of elemental forces when intense emotion sublimates the raw character of the Western landscapes.

*The chill white waters of the Tuolumne River tumble over slopes planed smooth
by the glaciers whereas the still waters of the Merced mirror the towering granite walls of El Capitan.
Yosemite National Park, California.*

6

ALASKA

The big country

"As wild and as pure as paradise...
where everything was found in profusion,
in quality and quantity to satisfy the gods and men."

John Muir,
American writer, philosopher and naturalist (1838-1914)

Southern Alaska is a calving ground for the glaciers
◁ *which gouge these deep fjords as they inch their way to the sea.*
Kenai Fjords National Park.

*Taiga ponds alternate with thinning conifer forests
in the region of Peters Creek Country.*

Stretching to within practically a mile of the Russian border, the huge peninsula of Alaska is the largest of all the United States of America. Indeed, the Alaskans teasingly refer to all the other states of the union as 'the small states'. With its 586,000 square miles, it covers an area equal to nearly one-fifth that of the rest of the United States. This land has been fractured by tectonic collisions, great tongues of ice have shaped and polished its turbulent topography and Alaska's volcanic islands have sometimes heated the ocean and whipped it to fury. Access to the self-styled 'Last Frontier' isn't easy, yet this harsh, austere land has attracted its share of intrepid settlers. Since the first human migrations, some 12,000 years ago, across the then land-bridge of the Bering Strait from Asia, adventurers have succeeded one another in waves, all attracted by this land of promise.

At the foot of the Talkeetna Mountains,
the scanty forests, peat bogs and lakes form a typical taiga landscape.

The huge moving mass of Hubbard Glacier crumples and fissures as it slowly inches into Disenchantment Bay.
Wrangell-St. Elias National Park.

GRANDEUR ON ANOTHER SCALE

Lapped by the Beaufort Sea and the Arctic Ocean to the north, the Bering Sea and the Chukchi Sea to the west and the Pacific Ocean to the south, the Alaskan coastline has been chiseled by ice, ravaged by volcanic eruptions, severed into countless

islands and cut open by racing torrents. The tidal shoreline winds over 34,000 miles, representing practically 40% of the total US coast. The state is dominated by the twin peaks of Mount McKinley, at 20,320 feet the highest mountain in North America. Of the twenty highest summits on North America, seventeen are to be found in Alaska. At the point where the Pacific continental plate runs in under Alaska, the subduction has given birth to the great undersea Aleutian trench, a curved depression plunging to more than 24,000 feet below the waves. Fencing the Pacific from the Bering Sea, the peaks of a chain of seabed volcanoes emerge as the Aleutian Islands. Measured from the seabed, 9300-foot Mount Shishaldin, on Unimak Island, in fact

culminates at over 32,000 feet, a good head higher than Everest. The south-eastern region has its own geographical excesses. Five thousand glaciers cover some 30,000 square miles of land and the greatest of them, the huge Malaspina Glacier, itself sprawls over 1100 square miles. Add to this three thousand rivers and torrents, three million lakes and a thousand islands - for the south-east alone - and we begin to understand why the state's name comes from a corruption of the Aleut word for 'great land'. What we imagine to be a land sleeping under an icy quilt, is in fact America's 'bad boy', racked by seismic tremors, huge landslides, tidal waves and volcanic eruptions. Several times in modern history, Alaska has made headlines with its violent volcanic activity. Here again the vast scale of the land asserts itself, as illustrated in the larger-than-life landscapes in the south and in the Aleutian Islands. Opposite Kodiak Island, the Katmai National Park protects the remains of the 1912 volcanic cataclysm which created the Valley of Ten Thousand Smokes. This strange valley opens, wide and bare, onto a vast reddish-ocher plain fringed with charcoal trees and is overlooked by a girdle of volcanic peaks like Mount Katmai. The tumbling waters of the Lethe, so-named from one of the two springs in the Greek mythological underworld, disappear into the volcanic ash and pumice. In early June 1912, growing tensions in the earth's crust shook the region. The earth opened and a new volcano, Novarupta, burst forth from the floor of the valley and threw out a torrent of incandescent sand and swirling gas. Three days later, when the hail abated, a thick, sterile blanket of sand covered the 70 square miles of the valley floor, annihilating all forms of life. For years afterwards, jets of gas and boiling steam issued from vents in this valley floor, some hot enough to set wood alight. When, three days after the eruption, Mount Katmai exploded, the effects on Kodiak Island and the mainland were catastrophic. Fish and shellfish died, triggering famine for the local population. The world's largest carnivores, the starving Kodiak bears, began to attack the local livestock. A cloud of ash was projected into the higher layers of the atmosphere and drifted around the world in the boreal latitudes. The triple peak of Mount Katmai had disappeared and when Robert Griggs, director of the National Geographic Society, discovered the valley three years later, he noted with astonishment that *"as far as the eye can see, the valley is*

Marine life abounds in these tidal pools left by the retreating waters of Cook Inlet.

*As the ice withdraws, pioneer plants and lichens move in
to colonize the sediment-rich crevasses in the rocks. Mendenhall Glacier.*

The eastern strip of Alaska, nicknamed the Panhandle,
is protected by the Tongass National Forest. The wild and often rocky coast, like Yakutat Bay,
is lashed by waves from the Gulf of Alaska.

filled with hundreds, thousands... no, what am I saying? with hundreds of thousands of smokes. It looks like all the steam engines in the world have come to meet here. ".

This great country is a composite of quite distinct regions, separated from one another by the imposing relief which, for each, determines the climate. The Brooks Range in the north, at over 3000 feet, is an extension of the Canadian Rockies. Its worn relief bears witness to ancient glacial action. Overlooking a wide plateau sloping down towards the Beaufort Sea, the Brooks are ravined with a network of watercourses. In these high continental latitudes, rainfall is light, the air dry and temperatures excessively low. These are the gates to the vast Arctic lands, to the realm of the permafrost and the tundra. The inland plateau, of moderate altitude, is deeply gouged by the watercourse of the mythical Yukon river, winding downwards to its huge delta on the Chukchi Sea. Tributaries running into the Yukon ramify over marshy plains known as 'flats'. The harsh, subarctic climate towards the center of the country limits vegetation to lichens and a sparse covering of tundra plants. Farther south, the Alaska Range, made up of volcanoes and rocky upthrusts, is much more recent but also much less stable. It shelters a coastal fringe splintered with islands before arcing like a bow down along the Alaska Peninsula and into the north Pacific in the form of the Aleutian Islands.

*Ready to fracture into icebergs,
the snout of Lamplugh Glacier refreshes the waters of Glacier Bay National Park.*

Uprooted by last winter's storms, polished by ice floes
and bleached by the salt waters of Icy Bay, these huge root systems lie stranded along the shoreline.
Wrangell-St. Elias National Park.

A LAND OF OPPORTUNITIES

During the Pleistocene epoch, when so much sea water was locked up in the polar icecaps, the Bering Strait became, on several occasions, a land bridge and the only entrance gate into America for, firstly, the animals, and later the first men. Bison, mastodons, musk oxen, caribou, moose, elk and other immigrants traveled through the long thick grass of the land connection, soon followed by the carnivores such as saber-toothed cats, jaguars and wolves. On the tracks of the animals came the stone age hunters, arriving in what would so many centuries later be baptised the New World. Archaeologists have still not come up with proof that the first Amerindians arrived on foot. Did they cross the strait in canoes or on ice floes at the only point where Alaska can be seen with the naked eye from Asia? Whatever their means of transport, three ethno-linguistic groups were settled in Alaska before the arrival of the white man: Indians, Aleuts and Eskimos. The Haida and Tlingit Indians inhabit the wooded south-eastern regions whereas the Athabascan live farther inland. The Aleuts, traditionally fishermen and hunters of marine mammals, have chosen to stay along the coast and out into the archipelagos. The last arrivals, the Eskimos (their Old Bering culture has been dated to around 300 BC), have spread over the rest of Alaska.

The first white man to beach on the coast of Alaska was a Dane named Vitus Jonassen Bering. Sighting the snowy summit of the St. Elias volcano, he first landed on Kayak Island in the summer of 1741, after having been appointed by Peter the Great seventeen years earlier to discover whether Asia and America were divided. Although the great navigator died on the return journey, his party brought back pelts of fur seals and sea otters, the first of the many riches this cold land of opportunity was to offer the intrepid. Attracted by these furs which were so light and yet so dense, the Russians rushed

to take over the bountiful hunting grounds of the Aleutian Islands. In the late spring of 1786, in the course of his seventeenth expedition, the Russian captain Gerassim Pribilof had been navigating blind in a thick milky sea-fog for several days when suddenly he heard a distant murmer which rose to a clamor as he approached. Georges Blond, in his *La Vie Surprenante des Phoques*[5], relates the episode, "The fog suddenly lifted... The land was there, absolutely covered with a packed gray and brown mass, the mass of thousands of seals whose incessant calling fused into a continuous hub-bub. The seals regarded the men's arrival without suspicion... little knowing that man was to become their most cruel and implacable enemy.". The Russian hunters progressed from island to island, exterminating both the animals and the local peoples. As the Russian American Company declined, the Russians lost interest in this territory known as 'Russian America', their major preoccupations being focused on their western front and on the Crimean War, and began negotiations with Washington for the sale of the colony. These negotiations, delayed by the American Civil War, were finally concluded in 1867 for an agreed price of $7,200,000. Alaska, as it was now called, finally became the 49th American state in 1959. With this first onslaught, Alaska, the land of the brave, became the prey of the greedy. To save the fur seals from extinction, the federal government had to draw up legislation strictly limiting open-sea hunting before it was too late. The whalers then disembarked from New England, harpoons whetted for the right whales, the sperm whales and the walrus. Inland, trappers massacred the fur animals and decimated the fish, thereby depriving the Indians and the Aleutians of their staple source of nourishment. Gold fever drew a second wave of immigration when nuggets the size of beans were found in the Yukon river. Prospectors began

[5]*The Surprising Lives of Seals*

Progressing smoothly across the chill highlands,
this snake of ice rumples and hesitates as it reaches the lower slopes.
Henbert Glacier, Tongass National Forest.

Streaked with blues, the ice cliff takes its opalescence from the sky and the darker waters of Glacier Bay.
Seemingly immobile, it suddenly fractures and plunges into the sea with a deafening crash.

to dig, to strip and to sift the hitherto virgin land. The seam discovered in Bonanza Creek, a tributary of the Klondike river, attracted a rough, lawless breed of men from America, Canada and, later, Europe and Australia. The rush spread even farther northwards, bringing a population of 30,000 by the turn of the century. Sixty years later, a similar rush again threw the land into turmoil when men began

In southern Alaska, the great glaciers left a waterlogged land in their wake, soon colonized by the forest.
Kadashan Creek Pool, Chichagaf Island, Tongass National Forest.

Temperate rain forests of conifers thrive in the warmer south of the state, the region with the highest rainfall. ▷
Tongass National Forest.

to prospect, drill and pump the black gold it contained. Oil drilling on a large scale began on the Kenai Peninsula in 1961 and the potential of the Prudhoe Bay strike is estimated at 10 billion barrels, in other words more than a quarter of the entire United States' production. To pipe this oil from the north down to the port of Valdez, the world's

up in 1910 to protect the Tlingit Indian culture and preserve the traces of the early Russian trading post (Sitka, capital of Alaska from 1867 to 1906, was formerly known as New Archangel). This was soon followed by the creation of other national parks and monuments: Mount McKinley in 1917, Katmai in 1918 and Glacier Bay in 1925. After nine years of

greatest private construction has been built. A rigid, somewhat surreal-looking pipe zig-zags its way across the tundra, an 800-mile line of metal equipped with heating tubes against icy arctic weather and hung sometimes 10 feet above the ground to allow bears and other Alaskan animals to move freely across their traditional ranges. The pipeline construction, with the financial compensations paid by the oil corporations for the damage it entailed, in fact helped to accelerate the settlement of the long battle the native populations fought to recover their land rights. With its transfer to the American camp in 1867, Alaska allowed America's wilderness conservation movement to gain momentum. The Sitka national monument, a 54 acre natural park, was set

discussions, research and planning, the American congress finally voted the Alaska National Interest Lands Conservation Act in 1980. This legislation created, extended or upgraded eight National Parks, two national Monuments and ten new natural preserves (administered by the National Park Service) where hunting and trapping are still allowed. This act also lent support to local populations, encouraging them to continue traditional subsistence activities such as hunting, fishing and gathering. National parkland in Alaska was doubled in one legislative stroke and now covered some 13% of the state. The Wrangell-St. Elias park, with its 8.3 million acres, is now the Park System's largest area, practically four times the size of Yellowstone.

The majestic Matanuska Glacier wends its way down from the Chugach Mountains.

This sunlit glade in the Tongass National Forest shows another side to the Alaska we usually imagine.

FROM ICEBERG TO FOREST

Pushed irresistibly down from their mountain fastnesses, the glaciers surge, open-mawed, into the cold waters of the ocean. The glittering translucid ice face, several hundred meters high and studded with dark stones torn from the mountain slopes, reflects the colors of the sky and the sea. From the immaculate white peaks of their birth, they snake their way slowly but inexorably down the slopes. Their skins furrow, split and blister on the way, cracking into gaping crevasses which act as funnels for churning meltwater. They strip the earth like graders and leave the rocks planed and smoothed. As the shoreline approaches, they accelerate to their death, fracture, explode and plunge into the sea, generating tidal waves with their weight. Now icebergs, they drift at the mercy of the waves, molded by the heat of the ocean and the erosive force of the winds. Thrown up on a beach, their ephemeral beauty trickles, drop by drop, into oblivion. The landscapes of the Alexander archipelago down in the Panhandle, like those of the Columbia river bay, were carved and fashioned by

the icecap which once covered the entire Arctic. The pre-ice age vegetation is beginning to reappear. A clump of black peat, mulched with moss and scouring rush, forms a starting point. The thick mattress of dryas, one of the hardiest plants, is pushed aside thirty-five years later by an alder. The alder is then outstripped by a poplar, which stunts it by depriving it of light. Both are later overshadowed by a spruce. Finally, as last link in the chain, comes the towering hemlock, the evergreen *Tsuga,* backbone of the magnificent damp forests of southern Alaska. The uneven ground, thickly carpeted with moss, combines with the dark, dense undergrowth to make walking difficult. Moss clings to the roots and trunks of the trees, lichens hang in garlands from the branches and the filtered light illuminates a symphony of greens.

*Young pines and hemlocks reach for the sky in the Tongass Forest
while mosses droop from the rain forest conifers in the Russel Fjord Wilderness.*

LICHENS, MOSSES AND SAXIFRAGES

Bent by the north wind, flattened by a thick mantle of snow, frozen by the searing cold and starved of light, Arctic vegetation has had to learn to adapt. As first settlers in this virgin landscape, the lichens are past masters in the art of survival, so much so that some are a respectable 4000 years old. Unencumbered by roots, stems or

leaves, these primitive plants thrive with only a bare branch or naked stone to support them. Others require no support at all, living free lives wherever the wind blows them. Lichens are in fact composed of two plant forms growing in so close a symbiotic association that they seem one single entity: an alga containing chlorophyll and a fungus supplying water and mineral salts. They grow extraordinarily slowly, at a rate of barely five millimeters a year, but neither the great droughts nor the bitter cold can discourage them. Even older, the mosses play an essential role

in the rebirth of the vegetation. Soft and velvety, they wither without dying during the great droughts. At the first signs of spring, the purple saxifrage begins its annual race against the threat of bad weather. In less than a month, it shoots up, flowers and spreads its seeds, growing in clumps scarcely three to five centimeters high on generally damp and rocky ground. Its many tiny leaves, pressed against one another, increase the plant's photosynthetic capacities.

Despite the short arctic summer,
the hardy wildflowers still manage to bloom, changing the face of this often-austere land.
Glacier Bay and Kenai Fjords National Parks.

THE TUNDRA

Above the southern shoreline of Alaska, the cold never relinquishes its grip on the land, even in the height of summer when the light barely fades. The subzero average annual temperature determines both plant and animal life. The entire landscape is covered with a specifically Arctic vegetation, the tundra. The word conjures up pictures of emptyness and sterility for many of us but in fact the tundra, a subtle blend of vastness and intimacy, of fragility and endurance, is cloaked with a sweet, austere beauty in all seasons. Every summer, when the cold gives way to the pale sunlight, flowers bring fresh color to the waxy cheeks of the landscape. Fall feeds the animals and birds with a host of berries hidden under a blanket of russet leaves. As far as the eye can see, the tundra ignites into an ocean of fire with the contrasting yellows, ochers, oranges and deep browns of the the vegetation. The Arctic wildlife also changes with the seasons, adapting to life on the tundra. During the long winter months, in their struggle against the cold and predators, most animals turn into ghosts with snowy pelts or plumage. In the spring, the caribou begin their migration north, feeding as they go, into the kingdom of the grizzly.

Inland from the southern coast, the tundra begins. Bog plants turn ocher, yellow and rust-red in the early fall,
a season when this vegetation also produces a profusion of wild berries.

THE GRIZZLY, A SOLITARY WANDERER ON THE TUNDRA

Motionless in the icy water, balanced on a slippery rock, muzzle outstretched and eyes riveted on a tumbling waterfall, the great bear has been waiting for hours to catch one of the leaping salmon which battle against the current of the Brooks River. Summer has arrived in Alaska. Every stream and river is alive with an endless, teeming migration of salmon following the age-old paths to their spawning grounds. And while the salmon concentrate their energies in surmounting the falls, leaping six feet with a flick of their powerful tail fins, the grizzlies are already in place for this annual rendez-vous. And thus the carnage of the short arctic summer begins. Each bear has developed its own fishing strategy. Some wait with infinite patience until the salmon ventures within reach of a lightning paw. The youngsters plunge full-length into the river, necks outstretched to catch the fish in their jaws, while others adopt the amusing tactic of wading through the river or lake with their head underwater, ready to hurl themselves open-mawed at the first flash of silver scales. The size of brown bears varies according to their diet. In the

tundra regions, this diet is low on meat, composed mainly of herbage, roots and berries supplemented with small mammals and the occasional caribou. In the region of the lakes and rivers, it becomes extremely rich in protein during the four to eight-week salmon season. The largest grizzlies are found, drawn in huge numbers by this summer fishing, within the Katmai National Park, the greatest sanctuary for brown bears in the United States today. On Kodiak Island, an adult male can stand nine feet tall and tip the scales at 1700 pounds. Eliminated from 98% of its former range since the conquest of the West, the grizzly owes its survival to the huge tracts of still untouched Alaskan wilderness, where its population is currently estimated at around 31,000. Grizzlies not only come in various sizes but also in a broad spectrum of colors ranging from pale caramel through cinnamon and fox red to dark brown or even mottled. This diversity, together with their ability to adapt to very different habitats, led 19th century naturalists to list up to 86 distinct species! Today's classification follows a reverse path and all brown bears have been grouped in one single species known as Ursus arctos. The name 'grizzly' is thus more descriptive than generic, derived from the peculiar 'grizzled' appearance of the bear's silver-tipped fur. With its massive head and humped shoulders, the grizzly looks heavy and clumsy. Appearances are deceptive, however, and potentially dangerous; grizzlies are surprisingly agile and fully capable, in bursts of 30 mph, of outsprinting a man. Supple, dexterous and equipped with long claws, bear paws are marvelous implements which can tear open a tree trunk, scoop and impale a slippery salmon or delicately gather fall berries. Each individual spends the summer and autumn months gorging to put on the reserves of fat necessary for four or five months of hibernation.

Alerted by some noise or unfamiliar smell, a grizzly rears up to try to locate the source.
Notoriously short-sighted, these bears rely much more heavily on their other senses.

Waiting to catch the migrating salmon with a snap of their jaws,
the bears stand upstream of the waterfalls of the Brooks River in the Katmai National Park.
These omnivorous wanderers also fatten for the winter on autumn berries,
roots and small rodents.

DENALI

THE GREAT ONE

The highest summit in North America is a camera-shy star, putting in brief appearances only when its mantle of clouds lifts momentarily. Created some 60 million years ago by a collision between two tectonic plates, Mount McKinley rises in one single upthrust from a wooded plateau barely 1500 feet above sea level and offers a towering 20,320-foot challenge to mountaineers. The Mount McKinley National Park was originally created in 1917 as a measure to save the wild white Dall sheep from the threat of extinction from over-intensive hunting. Enlarged and renamed by act of congress in 1980, the Denali Park now covers over four and a half million acres of the central part of Alaska, preserving and safeguarding a subarctic environment of high mountains, tundra and taiga and the great diversity of plant and wildlife it contains.

*A rare glimpse of Denali, the Great One, usually shrouded in a cloak of cloud,
surveying the magnificent fall colors of his tundra realm.*

Lumberjacks and builders, the beavers sometimes also work as landscape architects,
changing the face of rivers and lakes with their dams. Denali National Park.

THE MOUNTAIN OF LEGENDS

The first Amerindians arrived in the Denali region around 12,000 years ago at the end of the last Ice Age, their hunters trailing the big game of the era: the mammoths, woolly rhinos, bison and reindeer. During the long summer days at this latitude, they watched the sun follow its daily course in an almost complete circle above the great mountains. Since it seemed to rise and set every day behind Denali, the Indians named the peak "the house of the sun". For the Athabascans, settled on the banks of the Yukon, the imposing Denali range was created in the course of a terrible battle between two mythical warriors, Totson and Yako, by the edge of a river; *"Totson hurled a magic spear at his rival but before it could reach its target, Yako turned a gigantic wave into stone as a rampart against the weapon."*. That petrified wave remained on the landscape, known today as Denali. Much later, towards the closing years of the 18th century, the English navigor George Vancouver is said to have glimpsed the 'Great Mountain' while cruising up the Cook Inlet. But at the time, and for many years to come, Mount St. Elias was thought the highest mountain in North America. Mount McKinley owes its name to the 25th president of the United States, William McKinley, and was named in his honor in 1896, a few months before he was elected, by a band of prospectors surveying the region for gold. Finally scaled in 1913, it now attracts hundreds of attempts each year but remains particularly dangerous because of its extreme climate. Denali the Great One remains a mountain of legends.

EASY ACCESS BUT STRICT PROTECTION

The Denali area owes its protection to the naturalist Charles Sheldon. He undertook several missions around the mountain and was the first to propose measures to save the caribou, the moose and the Dall sheep from the guns of the hunters. His efforts were rewarded in 1917 when the Mount McKinley National Park was created. For the first fifty years of its existence, innocent of any road suitable for motor vehicles, the park welcomed fewer than 150 visitors a year. But when, in 1960, the Anchorage-Fairbanks highway was opened, Denali soon became the most accessible and most popular park in Alaska. When the annual number of visitors swelled to 140,000, the Park Service began to worry seriously. What was the influence of a public road running for 100 miles through the park? How had the wildlife reacted to the creation of the road? It was originally intended to help visitors view the animals but now, as traffic jams increased, drove them away. The decision was then taken to have visitors leave their cars in a parking lot at the entrance to the park and to use old school buses to transport everyone free of charge around the park road. Most visitors remain on board but the more adventurous ask the driver to let them off on condition that they promise to respect the park ruling of staying at least 400 yards from the animals they watch. For these intrepid souls, the Yellow Buses are their only means of access to the freedom of the wilderness where they can escape for a few days, enjoying their freedom in the land of the bears. And here again, to limit human pressure on the environment, the Park Service has fixed a strict set of rules. Each backpacker, authorized with a camper's permit, can travel within the areas it allows. He must pack his food in 'bearproof' containers and trust in his topographical map to guide him across a landscape without any beaten trails.

Autumn spreads its russet mantle over Kesugi Ridge in the Denali National Park.

Like snow in summer,
arctic cotton blooms in the wetlands of Denali National Park.

The Denali region owes its protection to the naturalist Charles Sheldon who,
seeking to save the caribou and the Dall sheep from hunters' rifles, did the wolf a good turn too.

A freshwater pond ringed by the Chugach Mountains. Chugach National Forest.

THE BIG FIVE

In 1980, the Alaska National Interest Lands Conservation Act was voted by the US Congress. Under pressure from Alaskans who had never accepted the name of Mount McKinley, the National Park was rechristened Denali and, in the same year, saw its area tripled. Rules regarding tourist visits were made considerably tougher for the central section called 'Denali Wilderness' but within the peripheral zone the local populations were authorized to continue their traditional subsistence activities. The concentrated three-month duration of the Alaskan spring-summer-fall is a period of intense activity for most animals, a time when they must find food resources to see them through the interminable winter. For visitors, this is the ideal time to glimpse the famous 'big five', the five emblematic representatives of North American wild animals; the caribou, the moose, the wolf, the Dall sheep and the grizzly. Saved from probable extinction by the creation of the park,

the Dall sheep now roams in large flocks up the steepest slopes of the park. The ewes, entrusting their lambs to 'lamb-sitters', graze on the high alps while the males live separately in bachelor bands. Their numbers now exceed 1 000 within the park. Since its enlargement, the park now protects the entire migration range for the caribou, from the fawning regions to the winter refuges. The Denali herd, one of the fifteen which crisscross Alaska, is estimated at between two to three thousand head. The best time to see or photograph them is the late summer period when groups of six to a dozen individuals begin to band together for the fall migration. While the caribou cross the entire territory, the moose remain in the aquatic zones where the long grass and the willow shoots form the staples of their diet. Of the mythical Big Five in Denali, the wolf is certainly the most difficult to observe yet he plays a role of primordial importance in the ecology of the park because of his position of principal predator. The wolf population in Denali is estimated at 160. In winter, they hunt mainly in packs but in summer, when small mammals abound, the wolf resumes his solitary hunting. Sometimes he can be seen at the side of a trail, sniffing the burrows of the woodchucks. As for the grizzlies, they are to be found everywhere, in all sorts of country. Their numbers are reckoned to be somewhere between two and three thousand within the park and the presence of these two super-predators, the wolf and the grizzly, is seen as a sign of the excellent ecological balance of the natural environment, notwithstanding the presence of man. The Denali National Park has also received recognition as a Natural Biosphere.

Sunset over Jefferies Glacier in the Wrangell-St. Elias National Park.

As sedimentary layers are washed away,
these petrified trunks of a bygone forest of gigantic trees rediscover the Arizona sky.
Petrified Forest National Park.

c o n c l u s i o n

In the late 19th century, two opposing currents divided the environmental movement. John Muir and his supporters wanted to protect nature for aesthetic reasons whereas Gifford Pinchot and his faction defended the idea of resource management. These two approaches still divide environmentalists today, both in the United States and in other developed countries, raising questions of interpretation and intention. In creating the national parks, the Americans thought they could preserve natural environments for the benefit of mankind. This system of protection has become a worldwide model and the parks have enjoyed an ever-increasing popularity since their creation. The price of this success, tourist overpopulation, has created unexpected problems of destruction of natural habitat and disturbance of animal life. Nature in the parks is far from pristine and pollution now rears its ugly head. Over five million tourists visit the Grand Canyon every year, eight hundred thousand of them in clattering helicopter flyovers. Visitor pressure has become so overwhelming in Zion that the idea of closing the park to the public has been considered. Animals have become semi-domesticated by visitors whose presence has imperceptibly modified the infinitely delicate ecological balance despite all protection measures. These magnificent islands of protected wilderness are subjected to many external influences. Among the 1750 types of threat listed by the National Park Service, the most common dangers are the dissemination of exotic plants and the invasion of exogenous animal species. The Florida swamps, surrounded by farmland, are the first to be affected by the pesticides and fertilizers carried in the runoff water. The Alaskan forests next to the parks are shipped off to Japan in pulp form. As everywhere in the world, untouched natural landscapes are being divided up, cut off from one another and thus deprived of the exchanges which enrich the biodiversity of the ecosystems. The national parks have had to resort to restoring environments and reintroducing species in order to continue their work and fulfil their protective role. With an annual budget of under one and a half million dollars, the Park Service is unable to fund all the programs needed to limit human impact on their lands and educate visitors. This is the challenge that has to be met if we are to restore our wildernesses in application of Thoreau's dictum that "in wildness is the preservation of the world.".

All the photographs in this book were taken by David Muench, except those by :

- *Joseph Muench : pages 16, 24, 25, 42, 43, 54, 55*
- *Bonnie Muench : page 99 (lower)*
- *Marc Muench : pages 23, 41, 46, 47 (right and left),*
          93, 95, 116,151, 174, 180 (lower), 231,
          240, 247, 262, 271, 282, 283
- *Explorer : page 17*
- *Explorer / Moisnard : page 20*
- *Explorer / T.M.C Hugh : page 21*
- *Explorer / Mary Evans : pages 26, 27*
- *Meinzer / Arnold / Bios : page 210*
- *Weimann / Bios : page 211*
- *Lusloos / Bios : page 245*
- *Mangelsen / Arno / Bios : page 274*
- *Klein / Hubert / Bios : pages 275, 280 (right and left)*
- *Munoz / Bios : page 280*
- *Alcalay / Bios : page 280*
- *Valarcher / Bios : page 280*
- *The Thomas Gilcrease Institute / Thomas Moran : page 38*

---

*"I would like to give special thanks and appreciation to the Nature Conservancy, Sierra Club,
Wilderness Society, Audubon, National Wildlife Federation and National Parks and
Conservation for their super efforts of preservation and stewardship of America's wilderness,
especially within the national parks."*

David Muench

*I'd like to extend my warmest thanks to the friends who supported me while I was working on this book,
to Georges Dumas and to Jacqueline and Bernard Dupuis for their enlightened geographical advice,
their research files, their kindness and their humor, to Nicole Vallée and to Andy Millar for their attentive
rereading of the manuscript and their suggestions, and especially to Olivier Grunewald, with whom I've
traveled across the endless North American landscapes for the last fifteen years,
always fueled by the same passion.*

Bernadette Gilbertas

Design and graphis
Elsa Hallak
BOWER
3 place aux Huiles - 13001 Marseilles, France

Photocomposition - photoengraving - and cartography
PLEIN FORMAT
72 boulevard Notre Dame - 13006 Marseilles, France

Printing
EGEDSA
Rois de Corella, 12-16, Nave 1
08205 Sabadell / Barcelone, Spain

© 2000
VILO
25 rue Ginoux - 75015 Paris, France

Printed edition February 2000
Legal inscription March 2000
ISBN 2-84576-011-6